UNDERSTANDING
REALITY
THERAPY

Also by Robert E. Wubbolding

USING REALITY THERAPY

UNDERSTANDING REALITY THERAPY

A Metaphorical Approach

ROBERT E. WUBBOLDING

Harper Perennial
A Division of HarperCollins*Publishers*

FIRST EDITION

Designed by Ruth Kolbert

Library of Congress Cataloging-in-Publication Data

Wubbolding, Robert E.
   Understanding reality therapy : a metaphorical approach /
   Robert E. Wubbolding.—1st HarperPerennial ed.
      p.   cm.
   Includes bibliographical references.
   ISBN 0-06-096572-X (pbk.)
   1. Reality therapy.   2. Metaphor—Therapeutic use.   I. Title.
RC489.R37W828   1991
616.89′14—dc20   90-55519

   01 00 99   RRD   10 9 8 7

CONTENTS

ACKNOWLEDGMENTS

Bill and Naomi Glasser have been
friends and helpers to me for many
years. They deserve gratitude
beyond what I can describe.
The best to both of you, today
and always. My wife, Sandie, has
provided me with encouragement,
belonging, and assistance in ways too
numerous to mention.
To you, "a thousand thank-yous."

FOREWORD

A problem is an
opportunity in work clothes.
—Henry Kaiser

This book is the result of five years of listening, collecting, teaching, and evaluating. The metaphors and stories contained in it were gathered from my experience with clients and workshop participants, as well as from extensive reading. They have been selected after trial and error in using them to illustrate and apply the principles of Control Theory as developed by William A. Glasser, and the principles of Reality Therapy.

The purpose of this book is to help the reader understand more deeply the principles behind Control Theory and the techniques of Reality Therapy. It is hoped that you will gain practical ideas for living a more satisfying life. A side effect will be that the reader's ability to listen will be greatly enhanced. Whether you are a professional person, a potential client, or someone wishing to be a more effective human

ix

being, you will hear in messages and statements language and conversations that you never heard before. At least, that is my experience since I became interested in metaphors about five years ago.

The use of metaphors, analogies, similes, and anecdotes can be eminently useful in the practice of therapy or any human communication, as well as in developing a self-improvement plan. As I write in Chapter 1, we are continuously using metaphors in our speech. In fact, our words themselves are metaphors. It seems only appropriate to understand and teach Reality Therapy by means of metaphors.

PREFACE

This enjoyable and interesting book contains dozens of brief metaphors and anecdotes that clarify and make understandable some of the most profound truths about human nature and about how to steer our behaviors toward more effective need fulfillment. These concrete and specific explanations extend the principles of Reality Therapy in ways that can be applied by the professional person to clients, patients, and students.

An even more significant contribution of this excellent volume is that Bob Wubbolding, my close associate, makes Reality Therapy usable for every person. When I developed the ideas of Control Theory and Reality Therapy, I aimed at making mental health accessible to the person in the street. I am proud to see that Bob Wubbolding has furthered this effort. In a previous book of outstanding quality, *Using*

Reality Therapy, he described the method clearly and precisely. In *Understanding Reality Therapy*, he has further concretized the priciples of Control Theory and Reality Therapy. I consider this book essential for grasping and implementing Reality Therapy and recommend it to all who seek to understand how to regulate their lives.

Wubbolding's metaphor "Radio Station WDEP" is his most important contribution in that it provides a system to help in understanding and using Reality Therapy. It is an eminently usable tool that can be learned by readers, used in agencies and schools, and taught in classrooms. I hope that this system will become a household phrase and used by therapists, counselors, teachers, and parents.

Finally, this book illustrates why several years ago I recruited Bob to serve as Training Director for the Institute for Reality Therapy. His experience as a professor at Xavier University as well as over two decades of counseling and training have helped him tap his creative imagination, a quality that is so needed in the helping professions.

William Glasser, M.D.

INTRODUCTION

Metaphors are keys which unlock a storehouse of ideas. The analogies, figures of speech, and anecdotes used in this book are intended to assist in the understanding, the practice, the teaching, and the living of Reality Therapy ideas. Therefore, the neophyte, the experienced practitioner, and everyone else can benefit from the ideas.

Some of the metaphors are more important than others. Thus, the "Cycle of Counseling," "Radio Station WDEP," the "$\frac{SAMIC^3}{P}$," and the "Mirror Technique" are most significant. While all of them are useful, readers are invited to judge which ones help them the most, and to complete the worksheet at the end of this book.

Some of the metaphors which William Glasser has used in his teaching of Control Theory are summarized here, and my own are elaborated in more detail. For more information, the reader is advised to consult the books which are listed in the bibliography. Nevertheless, a brief but adequate summary of "Picture Album," "Scales," "Behavioral Car," and "Two Filters" has been included and described from my own perspective.

It has been said that the best analogy limps, so too with metaphors, which are methods for explaining ideas. The reader is cautioned to see the counseling techniques as merely techniques, not as absolutes to be followed blindly. Thus, the example of "trying to stay awake" illustrates that sometimes a problem is not solved by confronting it directly. Rather, it is often more efficacious to encourage the problems to get worse. This is a technique to be used occasionally and within guidelines. Occasionally a baseball pitcher intentionally walks a batter. It is a strategy that can be used appropriately but should not be used indiscriminately.

It should be noted that I have used the words "counselor" and "therapist" interchangeably, as well as the words "counseling" and "therapy." In the world of the professions, it is probably wise to make necessary distinctions between these ideas. For this book, however, I have accepted the statement of C. H. Patterson (1974), "The differences between counseling and therapy exist in the minds of those who want them to exist rather than in fact." I have also used the words "parents," "teachers," "supervisors," and "helpers." The reason is that Reality Therapy is applicable to all human interactions, and I often simply refer to "the practitioner of Reality Therapy."

It should be noted that the beginning of each chapter contains a summary of the general concept discussed in that chapter. Thus, in Chapter 3, a general summary and explanation of the needs is provided. This is followed by metaphors which illustrate the many facets of each concept. The metaphorical treatment of Control Theory and Reality Therapy culminates in "Radio Station WDEP," which is the summary of the procedures used to bring to life the theory and practice of a revolutionary form of therapy developed by William Glasser.

1

Metaphors: Are They Real?

Winston Churchill once said that words are the only things that last forever. This comment perhaps overstated the importance of ideas and thoughts. Nevertheless, words are symbols for concepts or thoughts. Our thoughts, in turn, are representations of reality, and in this sense are metaphors. Words are also representations of our thoughts and therefore representations of the reality itself. Thus "chair" is a word that represents the reality, more specifically the object in the external world designated by the metaphor.

DEFINITION AND IMPORTANCE OF METAPHOR

Lakoff and Johnson (1980) define a metaphor as "understanding and experiencing one kind of thing in terms of another." The term as used here includes similes, analogies, anecdotes, and other figures of speech. The definition of metaphor, then, is not to be taken in a restrictive way. Rather, it is a broad term embracing many ideas.

Summarizing the importance of metaphors, Lakoff and Johnson state, "metaphor is pervasive in everyday life, not just in language, but in thought and action. Our ordinary conceptual system, in terms of which we both think and act, is fundamentally metaphorical in nature." They illustrate the pervasiveness of metaphor by the example of "argument is war," "argument is a building," and "argument is a container."

1. Argument as War:

Your claims are indefensible.
He attacked every weak point in my argument.
His criticisms were right on target.
I've never won an argument with him.
You disagree? Okay, shoot!
If you use that strategy, he'll wipe you out.
He shot down all my arguments.
We lost the argument.
He gave ground.
She took a new line of attack.

2. Argument as a Building:

We've got a framework for a solid argument.
If you don't support your argument with solid facts, the whole thing will collapse.
He is trying to buttress his argument with a lot of irrelevant facts, but it is still so shaky that it will easily fall apart under criticism.

With the groundwork you've got, you can construct a pretty strong argument.

3. Argument as a Container:

Your argument doesn't have much content.
That argument has holes in it.
You don't have much of an argument, but his objections have less substance.
Your argument is vacuous.
I'm tired of your empty arguments.
You won't find that idea in his arguments.
That conclusion falls out of my argument.
Your argument won't hold water.
These points are central to the argument—the rest are peripheral.
I still haven't gotten to the core of his argument.

EVERYDAY METAPHORS

He's on my back.
Can't shake him loose.
A breath of fresh air.
Cold as hell.
Pain in the neck.
Learn the ropes.
The situation heated up.
Roll over and play dead.
An upbeat sort of person.
My door is open.
He hit a home run.
She struck out.

Bite-size pieces.
Smiling on the inside.
Happy as a pig in slop.
Good times ahead.
Light at the end of tunnel.
Falling down.
Seeing the bright side.
Blank check.

The titles of movies are often metaphorical:
"Gone with the Wind"
"The Lost Weekend"
"A Star is Born"
"Down and Out in Beverly Hills"
"Star Wars"
"Rain Man"

USE OF METAPHOR IN COUNSELING

The use of metaphor in counseling and psychotherapy is also a current trend. Weeks and L'Abate (1982) speak of the importance of metaphor in Paradoxical Techniques. They describe alluding to mountain-climbing skills with a person who is experiencing anxiety at starting a new job. They add that "Erickson's best-known metaphor is that of talking about and prescribing dinner as a way to deal with sexual problems." DeShazer (1986) described guidelines for using metaphorical (paradoxical) tasks in family therapy.

Barker (1985) enumerates specific purposes of metaphors as they apply to counseling. He indicates that they can be used to suggest solutions, to help people recognize themselves (an indirect way to help them evaluate their behavior), to plant seeds for increasing motivation, to decrease resistance, and to redefine problems, to name a few.

BRAIN THEORY AND METAPHOR

Not only are metaphors used in the practice of counseling with clients, they are also useful in teaching the underlying theory and process to learners at any stage of their education.

In explaining how the human brain functions, it has been customary to utilize state-of-the-art technology. Over the years, the brain has been compared to a steam engine, a telephone switchboard, and a computer (Wubbolding, 1988). Thus, Wiener (1948), Powers (1973), and Pask (1975) use the current state of cybernetics as an analogy for the human brain.

In further developing Control Theory as a basis for Reality Therapy, Glasser (1984) has used an intricate series of metaphors. He speaks of a "Picture Album," "Scales," "Filters," and "Behavioral Car." It is clear that these analogies explain the phenomenon of human brain activity by comparing it to more easily understood concepts.

In the subsequent chapters of this book, I explain these metaphors and provide many others which are useful in understanding the theoretical basis of Reality Therapy, known as Control Theory or Control System Theory, as well as the principles and techniques of Reality Therapy itself.

Before each series of metaphors, I provide a more traditional and abstract summary of the concept. For example, the remainder of this chapter is a discussion of needs and metaphors related to each of them. Similarly, I explain the various kinds of evaluation and why it is useful in counseling. This is followed by metaphors which aid the understanding and practice of this central component of the "cycle of counseling."

CONVENTIONAL METAPHORS AND HUMAN NEEDS

Reality Therapy is based on the fundamental principle that we are motivated by five innate human forces. In all of our behavior we seek to fulfill these needs. Even negative behaviors, such as arguing, fighting, stealing, and killing are designed to meet these human needs. Although such behaviors are destructive, they nevertheless have a purpose in the mind of the person generating them.

These needs are general, not specific. We have specific wants, but no one has a *need* for a wife, a husband, a particular friend. Rather, we have general needs for belonging. Below are the five needs as described by Glasser (1986), as well as metaphors used in everyday speech related to each need. Though these metaphors are used in daily conversation, their meaning could be easily ascertained the first time someone hears them.

1. *Belonging:* the need for involvement with people; the need to love and be loved, to affiliate and bond with other people.

   BELONGING
   He knows everyone in town.
   He's a back-slapper.

She's a warm person.
He's a ball of fire.
She's like a recluse.
He turns me off.
She has a magnetic personality.
He has a winning smile.
Smile, your face won't break.
She had a faraway look.
He chewed me out.
Has a cat got your tongue?

2. *Power:* The need for achievement and accomplishment. Everyone has a need to feel a sense of being in charge of his/her own life.

POWER and ACHIEVEMENT
He knows his field inside and out.
She's as smart as a whip.
He was gunning for me.
She's playing one-upmanship.
He's a loose cannon.
He was all over the place in his lecture.
I'm lost when I study this subject.
I'm nowhere with this project.
He can't see the forest for the trees.
I learned the ropes.
I'm no longer the new kid on the block.
He learned it A to Z.
She's got the Midas touch.
He's as rich as Croesus.
She didn't know which way was up.
He's as stubborn as a mule.
She has drive.

3. *Fun.* The need to enjoy life, to laugh, to see humor.

FUN
I was tickled pink.
I got a kick out of your comment.
It was a side-splitting story.
I feel new again.
He was down in the dumps.
My job is a pain in the neck.
He has lost interest in his work.
We had a ball at your house.
I felt as low as a snake's belly.

4. *Freedom:* The need to make choices, to live without undue restraints.

FREEDOM
She's free as a bird.
I'm tied up tonight.
His wings were clipped.
Things are closing in on me.
He's a slave to his schedule.
She had a change of heart.
There was no way out.
I'll shake loose for a few hours.
I feel like a bird in a cage.
You can breathe easy now.

5. *Survival:* The need to maintain life and good health. This need includes the sub-needs for comfort, food, air, etc.

SURVIVAL, PHYSIOLOGY
She's a walking time bomb.

He's as healthy as a horse.
She had deep brown eyes.
Lean as a rail.
He's built like a fireplug.
Her health is going downhill.
He could whip his weight in wildcats.

It is evident that ordinary words and phrases are often metaphorical and their meanings rarely need to be explained. Most people quickly learn and never forget the meaning of these commonplace metaphors. Moreover, they can be related to the human needs that lie at the root of all human motivation. Chapter 3 contains a description of detailed metaphors as they relate to the understanding of each need.

2

Preliminary Metaphors

The metaphors used in Reality Therapy, with the exception of those used in this chapter, are grouped together according to the various aspects of the control system and the methodology of counseling from the Reality Therapy perspective.

Introduction: Expectations of Workshop
Participants and Trainees

Control Theory/Background
    Needs
    Wants
    Behavior
    Perceived World and Perception

Reality Therapy/Delivery System
    Environment: Establishing the Relationship

Procedures: Direction/Doing
Procedure: Evaluation
Procedure Planning
    All procedures

INTRODUCING CONTROL THEORY
AND REALITY THERAPY; EXPLORING EXPECTATIONS

In order to understand the concepts of Reality Therapy, I would like to begin by describing in detail an activity that is used in my training workshops. You can use it at home with your family, at work with your staff, or you could adapt it to yourself for private use. It is an exploration of the participants' hopes and desires for the program, i.e., what they want to "get out of the training." It is useful to have each person write down what they want to learn as a result of the training. The importance of this activity should be stressed, though their grasp of its significance becomes more complete after they understand the nature of the Control Theory. They are asked to discuss their training goals (wants) in small groups for fifteen to twenty minutes. Then they are asked to make a group list on flip chart paper which is posted for all to see. The leader should explain that there are several purposes to this important exercise.

a)   It is a warm-up activity that serves to help them get from "there and then" to "here and now." Many participants are undoubtedly somewhat distracted, preoccupied, or apprehensive as they start this new experience, often away from home or in unfamiliar surroundings. Such an activity helps them to relax and attend more closely to the training program.

b)   It serves as an involvement activity at an intellectual level. Since it involves little emotional self-disclosure, it is viewed as safe and easy to do. Furthermore, talking about training expectations facilitates the lowering of personal barriers and enhances the trainees' inclusion in the group.

c) It provides an opportunity for the leader to model his/her style to the group and to teach by way of "Concomitant Learning" a valuable lesson (Concomitant Learning is what is learned as a side effect, i.e., as a lesson secondary to that which is first intended). The participants learn that there is a leader in charge, that there will be serious content to the program, that the leader will set an agenda, that their participation is expected, that the leader will attempt to balance small group participation and large group lecture/discussion, and that the leader has a sense of where he/she wants to take the students.

d) It is an indirect way to introduce a practical idea to the participants in the first hour of the program. The leader points out that it is important to ask clients individually or in groups about their wants. It is an idea that the participants can use immediately on their jobs, with their families, and in all their relationships. If they are teachers, or if they supervise groups or manage employees, they can incorporate this activity into their work setting. Rather than merely telling them about the importance of exploring the clients' wants or picture albums, the leader models the exploration by infusing the idea into the training itself. The credibility of both the leader and the ideas themselves is increased if the trainer demonstrates from the very start that the ideas can be used in the training as well as in therapy.

e) It provides structure for the teacher-student relationship. When the participants have posted their expectations, the leader reviews them quickly and describes which can be addressed and which are beyond the scope of the workshop. Some participants seek primarily their own personal growth as a "want" for the workshop. I have found it useful to explain that while personal growth is often a side effect of the program, it is not the focus. There are other sessions which aim at personal growth. The emphasis in the present program will be on growing professionally, increasing knowledge, and building skills. Thus, a later explanation will focus on the importance of and the ways for structuring the counseling relationship. Now, however, the teacher-learner relationship is structured by suggesting, for example, that "we will address expectations 1, 2, 5, 6, 7 on the flip chart, but numbers 3 and 4 relate more to personal growth and therefore they will not be emphasized."

f) It enables the leader to encourage the participants to have high expectations, yet recognize that in a few days or hours, they will not be able to solve all their problems. Still, they could very likely derive several (or many) practical ideas that would help them change their professional behavior to some degree. Thus the first metaphor is:

1. RAISING YOUR BODY TEMPERATURE FIVE DEGREES OR FIVE PERCENT

If, as a result of the training or learning of Reality Therapy through this book, a trainee, or you, the reader, would increase your effectiveness a mere five percent, you would derive a benefit which is quite noticeable. Analogously, if you were to raise your body temperature a mere five percent or five degrees, you would certainly notice it. A fever of 103° prevents a person from functioning. Thus, a change of five percent is an enormous change. You will notice a change in your professional, personal, and family behavior if you persist in the use of even a few of the ideas taught during a workshop or contained in this book.

You could, in fact, increase your effectiveness far more, but I am attempting to practice what Woody (1988) calls "onedownmanship." To hold out unrealistic "cures" or guarantees, to make promises that are often seen as outlandish, not only opens oneself to accusations of unethical behavior, but also undermines the credibility of an otherwise solidly grounded training and reading experience.

2. GOD IN A BOX

In understanding Reality Therapy, it is useful to realize that the principles of Reality Therapy comprise one very effective way to improve your own life or to counsel, parent, supervise, and deal with people. But they are not the only way. There are many theories of human behavior and they all have something to offer the student of therapy and counseling. The reader should know that the topic of this book, Reality Therapy, is not a closed system or a cult that a person blindly accepts in its totality. Thus, if you find part of the theory or method unacceptable, leave it aside and try to utilize those parts that fit with your own personal or professional philosophy and values.

As a teacher of Reality Therapy I have no corner on truth. It's been said that "truth is where you find it." The "God in a Box" metaphor implies that no one has God imprisoned in their teaching. No theory should be seen as containing "the truth, the whole truth, and nothing but the truth." Neither Reality Therapy nor any other theory has the almighty (universal and immutable truth, the answers to all the questions of life, the secrets to the universe) locked in.

The value in taking this nondefensive attitude is quite paradoxical. Once you see the nondogmatic approach to human behavior, even if you are adamant in your rejection of the principles, you will probably be able to sit back, relax, and open your mind to them. I once had a workshop participant say that she was far more open to Reality Therapy when she heard me say that one of my favorite books was Irving Stone's life of Freud, *Passions of the Mind*.

In a similar vein, it is useful to realize that Reality Therapy is both similar to and different from other theories of therapy and human behavior. For instance, Rational-Emotive Therapy denies that we have needs, yet in Reality Therapy we often deal directly with a person's thinking behaviors. Also, Adlerian counseling is based on the client's need for power. The Self Theory of Rogers aims at identifying the clients' inner incongruencies; it does not merely encourage an aimless wallowing in feeling as is often thought.

It is also helpful to know the connection between Reality Therapy and family counseling. This is explored elsewhere (Wubbolding, 1990b). It is sufficient to state here that Reality Therapy has many aspects that are comparable with Satir's communication theory as well as structural and strategic family counseling.

Finally, the most important point here is not that the ideas of Reality Therapy are similar or different from other theories and methods. The most significant point is that if you will find the ideas helpful in understanding Control Theory and Reality Therapy, use them, add to them, and leave aside whatever does not fit into your own wants and perceptions.

3. FOUR WINDOWS

In his classes at Cleveland State University, my friend David Santoro describes four windows to the human psyche. Each one has its own unique validity.

a)   Human beings can be seen through the medical window. In fact, one ethical responsibility of a counselor is to ensure that the client receives proper medical help. If a client has not had a physical checkup and is experiencing pain, he/she should be referred for medical help. Even Norman Cousins (1976, 1980), who took control of his own ill health, insists on the need for good medical treatment, and if you wish to apply these ideas to your own life, be sure to seek good medical help if you feel you are in need of it.

b)   The nutritional window also provides an entrance into the human psyche and a way to view human behavior. In an age when scientific evidence increasingly supports the importance of the need for good dietary habits and the use of food supplements, it is advantageous for counselors to include nutrition as an area for counseling. You might keep a written record of your own food intake and examine it to determine if your eating is what it should be.

c)   A growing number of persons seeking help wish to explore the spiritual and religious aspect of their problems, decisions, and personal growth. Pastoral counselors and spiritual directors specialize in this form of counseling and often provide valuable training for counselors who lack the knowledge and skill in handling spiritual issues.

d)   The psychological/educational window provides the primary opening to human beings for the Reality Therapist and other counselors. It is evident that while Control Theory is a "biological, psychological explanation" (Glasser, 1986), the emphasis is on the psychological aspect of human motivation and behavior. The use of these principles accompanies a healthy "check-up from the neck up."

The importance of each window can be exaggerated. To see human beings exclusively from any single window leads to excesses. Dealing with a person only from the medical viewpoint is to fail to see that human beings are more than the intersections of their chemical elements. Thus, depression is a total behavior that the human brain generates as a total choice. Similarly, we are more than what we eat. And though it is less likely that the nutritional window is exaggerated, it is possible to overemphasize it and fail to recognize the other aspects of behavior. There is perhaps, at the present time, more of an inclination to see human beings from an exclusively spiritual point of view. Carried to extremes, this perspective leads to such opinions as that of the preacher who says that alcoholism is a moral problem and prayer alone will cure it, or that marriages go bad only because those involved did not take their religion seriously enough. An excessively narrow view of humankind leads to such exaggerations. So, too, the psychological/educational window can be over-applied. In Reality Therapy we believe that a person's overall life improves when he/she attains better control. Yet there are assaults such as viruses, etc., that need to be treated medically. There is the need for good nutrition. Indeed, many counselors from various psychological persuasions believe in the usefulness and even necessity of dealing with the spiritual problems of their clients. It was St. Augustine who said, "Our hearts are restless until they rest in You."

The effective Reality Therapist enters the realm of human

behavior from the psychological/educational window, but also recognizes that the human being must be dealt with as a unified organism with human needs that transcend any single "window."

4. THERMOSTAT

A thermostat is a control system similar to our brain. It generates behavior because it "wants" something from the world around it. It wants a perception, as determined by the thermometer, that the temperature of the room be maintained, say, at 72 degrees. It generates behavior, the running of the furnace or air conditioner, in order to maintain the perception it is seeking. It will drive its "behavioral system" even if the process is sabotaged from without. Thus, if someone holds a candle under the thermometer in the summer, the thermostat will drive the air conditioner without interruption until it breaks down, or the candle is removed.

A human being is like a thermostat. All people have wants related to needs. We want, for example, a particular friend—related to belonging—or we want to feel good at our jobs, which is related to power. More precisely, we want a perception that we have a friend or that we are adequate on the job. This control system can be sabotaged also. However, it is often sabotaged from within through drugs. A person can take drugs to get the illusion of being adequate. Also, a person can drive his/her behavioral system to the point of physical or emotional breakdown, or even psychosis.

The human brain is thus a control system similar to a thermostat that seeks to "control" or "regulate," through its behavior, the world around it.

3

Metaphors for Needs

The metaphors just discussed are used in the introductory section of the training program. The activities and comments surrounding them range in length of time from a few minutes to an hour. The exact amount of time depends on the length of the training workshop. The metaphors in this chapter relate to the discussion of an important component of the human control system: human needs.

We are all born with the five human needs. These are general drives which we seek to fulfill by each and every human behavior (Glasser, 1980, 1986).

1. Belonging: Everyone seeks to be involved with others. Even survival is difficult without some dependence on and interaction with others. In our society this need is expressed in several ways: social belong-

ing—we need friends; work-related belonging—we wish to feel we have a place in the world of work or to have our efforts appreciated; family belonging—we desire comfort in our relationships with family. When this need is not met, loneliness results.

2. Power or Achievement: People have an innate tendency to seek competence, to have a sense of achievement or accomplishment, to gain self-esteem and self-worth, and to be in charge of their own lives. When this need is unmet, the consequences are feelings of being out of control.

3. Fun or Enjoyment: We all seek at least a sense of satisfaction and often enjoyment. This is loosely called fun. When this need is not met, boredom and depression take over.

4. Freedom or Independence: People seek to be able to run their own lives, to make choices unrestrictedly. They seek to act on their own without coercion. When this need is denied, the outcome is a feeling of being trapped, a sense of frustration and feelings of rebellion.

5. Survival: We all have a need to maintain life and to sustain health. This need is the basis for the smooth functioning of our basic physiology. Because of the need for survival our various inner systems function: digestion, blood circulation, etc.

These five needs are the sources of motivation and have the following characteristics (Wubbolding, 1985):

1. Innate: They do not need to be learned; we are born with them.

2. Universal: All human beings possess them; they cross all cultures.
3. General: They are not specific. Wants are specific and unique.
4. Overlapping: The fulfillment of one often is the fulfillment of another, e.g., having fun with another person.
5. Intraconflictual: Sometimes fulfilling one need means denying the fulfillment of another.
6. Interpersonally conflictual: Often the fulfillment of a need conflicts with the fulfillment of another person's needs.

Control Theory is based on the principle that people are motivated to fulfill a current force inside of them. This can be more controversial than is at first apparent in that early childhood conflicts, unconscious reasons, and external stimuli do not cause present behavior. Our motivation is *hic et nunc* (here and now).

5. RADIO STATION WII-FM

A basic principle of Control Theory is that the motivation and causality of behavior originate from within a person. Human actions, feelings, and thoughts are not the result of external stimuli. Rather, we all seek to fulfill the needs of Belonging, Power or Achievement, Fun or Enjoyment, Freedom or Independence, and Survival. Thus phrases like "a fit of depression came over me," "you make me mad," "my job causes me stress," "the weather gets me down," etc., indicate that the person ascribes control of his/her life to external causes, rather than to inner need fulfillment. As

21

Glasser (1986) has pointed out, "We are all internally motivated." In other words, we all live by the motto or listen to the radio station "WII-FM" ("What's In It For Me?").

Similarly, even our most altruistic behaviors are an attempt to satisfy our needs. This does not, however, lead to a cynical viewpoint of human nature. It merely implies that *all* behavior—even the most selfless and giving, the most generous and caring—is generated to satisfy something deep inside all of us.

6. LEGS OF A CHAIR

The needs should be seen as an interrelated system. As in any system, there should be balance among the components. This balance is achieved when each need is fulfilled proportionately and thus the system functions like the legs of a chair.

Any chair functions most effectively when there is balance among the legs. If one leg is too short or too long, the chair does not function very well. So, too, if a person seeks only to fulfill one need, sometimes the others remain unmet. Often we read about a well-known person, such as an athlete, who is effective at achieving and gaining power and recognition, but whose personal and family relationships are empty and shallow. Such a person *seems* to have a strong need for power and has chosen to donate a large proportion of his/her behaviors to its fulfillment.

On the other hand, in seeking need fulfillment, we need to maintain balance among the needs. At the same time, it is important to recognize that there are five legs to the chair. It is helpful to think of the chair as similar to a typist/secretary's chair, which has a central post (survival) from which spring the other four legs (belonging, power, fun, and freedom). In general, people seek survival as a need more fundamental than the others, yet it is often superseded or threatened by many people. Many individuals seek excitement such as skydiving, as a fun-need-fulfilling activity. This could well threaten their survival and some will even choose death or probable death in order to gain power or recognition. Boorstin (1968) describes the phenomenon of dueling, which was practiced in the United States until about the time of the Civil War: men dueled to preserve "honor" (power?). He cites dozens of famous people who dueled and who died rather than betray what they believed to be their "honor." The most well-known example, of course, is the duel in which Alexander Hamilton was killed by Aaron Burr.

In the present age, the outlawed practice of dueling has been replaced with equally harmful behaviors designed to increase power and competence. The reader is invited to generate examples.

Consequently, the metaphor about the legs of the chair can be discussed at length by the reader. It could be applied to historical figures and events, international relations, and personal experiences.

7. EMPTY SALAD BOWLS

Some founders of various theories of human behavior deny that we have human needs. They state, for example, that if we *needed* belonging, we would have it. Since we don't always have it, we don't need it.

Yet, in Reality Therapy, we do not teach that a need is something we always have. The opposite is what is suggested by those who subscribe to Reality Therapy. The human needs can be likened to large salad bowls which seek to be filled. A need is not something we always have, it is something we hope to have, or which we seek to maintain on a continual basis. Thus, our behavior serves the purpose of putting the salad into the salad bowl.

8. TAKE THE HILL

It's been said that in the "old army" when the sergeant told the troops to "take the hill," they followed the order without questioning it, and proceeded to take the hill. Glasser (1972) has described the world before approximately 1950 as "the Civilized Survival Society," in which people followed rules and laws simply because such behavior was the norm. Couples stayed married because divorce was less acceptable and not as widespread. Externals seemed to govern human behavior more completely than during subsequent decades. In the present society, the "Identity Society," people are more conscious of their psychological needs. In current western civilization, the survival need is of less concern than the identity need. People are more interested in who they are and whether the world is satisfying to them *now*. Thus, they are less controlled by externals. This explains how Reality Therapy, a theory and method that emphasizes human needs and internal motivation, has gained support and is widely practiced. It is based on principles congruent with this identity society: internal motivation, free choice, personal responsibility, self-determination, altruistic behavior, etc.

Even the U.S. military has attempted to incorporate the values and infrastructures of the identity society. There are equal opportunity and drug treatment programs. There are family counselors and management training. College degrees, even doctorates, can be gained while in the service. I once asked a chaplain who had seen many a battle how the military is different today than it had been in the past. His reply was, "We had the old army, the new army, and this damn thing." The military here is a metaphor for all of society. When the sergeant says "Take the hill," often the troops want to evaluate the advantages and disadvantages of owning the hill—before *they* decide whether they will *freely choose* to take it.

9. MICKEY RIVERS'S PHILOSOPHY

Mickey Rivers is known mostly for his lifetime batting average of .295 with the California Angels, the Texas Rangers, and the New York Yankees. He is less known for his philosophy and totally unknown for his study of Reality Therapy. Nevertheless, he is quoted by R. Bruce Dodd of the *Chicago Tribune* as reflecting a corollary to the principles of Reality Therapy and Control Theory:

> Ain't no sense in worrying about things you got control over, 'cause if you got control over them, ain't no sense worrying. And there ain't no sense worrying about things you got no control over, 'cause if you got no control over them, ain't no sense in worrying about them.

The bedrock principle of Control Theory is that behavior is an attempt to gain a sense of better control. The proficient use of the principles of Reality Therapy includes focusing on behaviors that can be changed and improved rather than on what cannot be effectively dealt with.

10. THOREAU'S AXE

In *Walden*, Thoreau describes his desire to be alone. To accomplish this, he journeyed to Walden Pond to build a retreat. One of his first decisions was to go down the road to borrow an axe in order to build a cabin. Paradoxically, it appears that being alone requires some dependence and involvement with others.

11. MY SPIDER

A counselor at a live-in school for court-referred adolescents told the story of a fifteen-year-old boy in his cottage who was seen by others as a "loner." He seemed to have few friends and showed little enthusiasm for group activities, yet he was reliable in doing his chores such as cleaning and sweeping. However, he neglected one part of his responsibilities: cleaning the outside of the window to his sleeping room. Finally, the cottage counselor took a broom and swept away the maze of spider webs that had accumulated on the outside of the window.

When the boy saw that this had occurred, he became very upset and sad. The counselor observed the boy's behavior and discussed it with him. The result was indeed startling. The boy told him, "My spider is gone. There was a large spider on the window that was my only friend. I would talk to it at night through the glass and now it is gone forever." The boy needed to grieve for the loss of his friend. This observant and sensitive counselor was astute enough to notice this process and to intervene in a positive manner and through several sessions helped the boy through the crisis. Incidentally, the counselor also needed assurance that the hurt he felt he inflicted was not only unintentional but temporary.

This story illustrates several important parts for learning and living the principles of Reality Therapy: people seek to fulfill a need for belonging in ways that are unique to each of them; other people may not perceive what is need-fulfilling and, with good intentions (wants), choose behaviors that impact on a person in ways that are totally unforeseen.

We all seek belonging in our own ways and what is satisfying to one person might be completely unnoticed by others. What implications does this have for you, your family, or your employer?

12. DUNCAN HINES DIFFERENCE

Weinberg (1985) describes how even some of the simplest actions can relate to power, and that people work to fulfill this need. After World War II, packaged cake mixes were introduced to the American public. He states that the mixes did not sell even though they required almost no effort—only that of baking after adding water. On the other hand, the Duncan Hines mixes vanished quickly from the shelves of stores. The difference in the Duncan Hines mixes was that they required the addition of an egg. The housewife could feel a sense of accomplishment "when she presented it to the family after supper, for she could truthfully answer, 'Yes, I baked it *myself!*' "

13. GLASSER'S POCKET DICTIONARY

In his speeches, William Glasser sometimes refers to a project he did while on vacation. He sat on a beach with a notebook and a pocket dictionary and categorized words according to the five needs. Thus, "important," "achievement," and "overwhelm" would relate to power. "Involved" and "gregarious" would pertain to belonging. "Enjoyable" and "ludicrous" would seem to come under fun. "Liberation" and "unrestricted" would be close to freedom. "Healthy" would come under the need for survival.

He found words relating to power to be fifteen times more numerous than any other need. The irony is that it is often difficult and even loathsome for people to admit to a need for power. Yet it motivates groups to assert themselves. It even motivates nations to exploit other nations. Still, it is difficult to say, "I have a strong need for power" or "I want more power." How do you seek power in your relationships?

14. THE POWER PIE

Fulfilling one's need for power should not be seen as exploitation of another person or diminishing someone else's power. There is no "power pie" which has only a limited number of pieces and which, therefore, symbolizes limited quantity. If such were the case, any gain by one person would mean a lessening of another's resources. One person's achievement need not take away that of another person. Power is an internal drive that can be measured by the inner satisfactions felt by one's own skills, abilities, and accomplishments, not by how one compares with others. When one person achieves a high level of skill as a golfer, comparisons will always be made, but genuine need-fulfillment results from the satisfaction that "I am the best golfer I can be."

15.   A FEW PIECES OF RIBBON

Napoleon once said, "I can make men die for a few pieces of ribbon." Some individuals choose death in order to achieve a sense of recognition and power.

16.   MICKEY MANTLE

The story is told about a noisy party in a hotel room on a rainy night. Mickey Mantle, retired from baseball for several years, was in attendance, and at one point was seen standing with his ear next to the window. When asked about this, he replied that he was listening to the rain hit the window. When queried about why, he said, "It sounds like applause."

Whether he missed the recognition he had received as a baseball superstar is not known. Nevertheless, this vignette serves as a metaphor to point out that recognition is desired and sought by human beings.

We expect our friends to greet us; we expect to be paid a respectable salary comparable to the work performed; we like to be complimented for our selection of clothes; we want to be thanked when we do someone a favor; and we rarely interrupt another person who is praising us.

Human beings want approval to varying degrees and some even seek it to a pathological degree. These extreme "people-pleasers" direct their every working hour to achieving the acclaim of others. As stated above (Legs of a Chair), the healthy person aims at balance in need-fulfillment. How have you shown recognition to others at work lately?

17.   5, 4, 3, 2, 1 MOST IMPORTANT WORD(S)

Ziglar (1989) describes the importance of recognition and respect by stating that the five most important words are "You did a good job." The four most important words are "Can I help you?" The three most important words are "Would you please?" The two most important words are "Thank you." And the single most important word is "You."

18.   PEAS AND CARROTS

I remember once when I was a small boy I refused to eat my dinner. For many children such a refusal is a way to fulfill a power need. After all, it is very difficult for parents to "force" their children to eat. In fact, trying to force them to eat generally results in a more obstinately rigid choice by the child. Though my mother never studied Reality Therapy, she understood the reality of human choice. And so my attempt to engage her in a power struggle ended abruptly because she effectively deflected the statement. She merely asked, "Which are you going to eat first, your peas or your carrots?" The best way to deal with a power struggle is to avoid it from the start. It is more helpful to give the person a choice and put the responsibility for the decision where it belongs.

19. ARISTOTLE'S DEFINITION

Fun is an innate human need. Babies seem to be naturally inclined to play and enjoy themselves. Parents teach children to work and discipline themselves, but they seek fun without guidance. Perhaps Aristotle recognized this when he defined a human being as a "risible" creature—a creature which can laugh.

20. BERLIN WALL–SPEED BUMP

The need for freedom is deep inside all human beings. It drives us to risk our lives and even give up our lives at times. The Berlin Wall will forever be a memorial to the misuse of power. It will be remembered as a symbol of how some people attempt to prevent others from fulfilling their need for freedom (and indeed all their needs).

In the autumn of 1989, the world witnessed the concerted efforts of millions of people in eastern Europe who no longer were willing to live with their unfulfilled need to make choices. The Berlin Wall, the barrier most symbolic of this "unfreedom," became merely a speed bump for those people journeying to freedom.

21. 100 VICTORIES

Would you like to get a surge of power without even talking to anyone and without even starting a new project or having a new success? Strange as it seems, you can do it. This can be done by following a suggestion of Ty Boyd (1990). Write down the phrase "100 victories" on a piece of paper. Then list 100 victories you have had in the last year. They can be minor or major accomplishments. It will help to stretch your mind if you don't repeat the same one twice. For instance, don't say "I got up early 30 times" and count that as 30 of the 100 victories. Push yourself to find 100 different victories or accomplishments—major or minor. If 100 seems to be overwhelming, start with ten. Then add another ten and go as far as you can. But remember, you can go a little farther with your numbers than you at first think you can.

22. CONGRATULATIONS

Many people have feelings of success and reasons to celebrate victories. Boyd (1990) suggests that if you randomly pick ten names from the phone book and send them a congratulatory note, eight of them would tie it to a real event in their lives. The lesson: look for your own success; life can be and *is* beautiful; count your blessings.

23. CURE FOR INSOMNIA

The cure for the negative symptoms of antisocial behavior, negative feelings such as depression, psychosis, psychosomatic pain, and addictions, is effective need-fulfillment. These negative symptoms are replaced by positive symptoms through the application of the "WDEP" system. The positive symptoms, the reverse of the negative, are described by Wubbolding (1988) as altruistic or contributing behaviors, positive feelings, rational thinking, healthful activities. This replacement of the destructive by the constructive is reminiscent of W.C. Fields's statement that "the cure of insomnia is to get more sleep."

4

Metaphors for Wants

We keep in our minds images of specific, desirable, need-satisfying perceptions. Glasser has referred to this as the "all we want world," and more recently as the "quality world" (1989, 1990). These images or wants are specific to each human being, related to each want, and sometimes in conflict with each other. These wants also serve to motivate specific human behaviors. Below are described in detail the characteristics of the inner world of wants.

A specific human behavior is generated when there is a discrepancy, difference, or gap between what we want and what we perceive we are getting from the world around us. This is further explained in detail by the metaphor "Out of Balance Scales."

24. PICTURE ALBUM

This metaphor, explained in detail by Glasser (1986a, 1986b), refers to the storehouse of perceptions that are seen as desired. It is part of the perceived world but is exclusively limited to those images that are need-fulfilling. There exist wants or pictures for each need. Wubbolding (1985, 1986) has described characteristics of the picture album.

a) Need-fulfilling; wants are related to needs.

b) Related to each sense; wants are related to touch, taste, etc.

c) Removable; wants can be replaced with other wants.

d) Realistically and unrealistically attainable; some wants can be fulfilled, others are beyond reach.

e) Specific; wants are precise, not general.

f) Unique; wants are unique to each person.

g) Blurred; wants can be unclear.

h) Prioritized; wants exist in levels of desirability.

i) Conflict with each other; wants can be mutually exclusive.

j) Conflict with others' wants; wants can create interpersonal problems.

k) Linked with each other; a want is desired because it is connected with another desired object.

l) Remote and immediate; wants can be sought after now or used at a later time.

m) Reminiscent; a want can be desirable because it reminds a person of another desired want.

One of the most important characteristics of the mental picture album is that wants or pictures are present in levels of intensity. In other words, their desirability is present in degrees. Some objects are seen as more desirable than others.

It is useful to determine the degree of intensity of our want, i.e., how much is the want desired or how "serious" are we about the specific want. The list below is a complete list. Still, it is not necessary to categorize the wants precisely in a rigid manner. It is often useful, for instance, to merely ask, "How badly do I want it?" "Is my want a nonnegotiable desire or weak whim?" "Is it something I intend to pursue relentlessly or is it something that 'would be nice to have?'" Nevertheless, the list below is an attempt to describe a complete spectrum of picture (want) desirability:

a) Nonnegotiable Demand—Desire for air, food, etc.

b) Pursued Goal—A want backed up by a behavior. Going to school, developing a relationship, getting a job or a promotion are examples. A more desirable want could replace them. In *Using Reality Therapy*, I have described five limits of commitment for achieving your wants.

c) Wish—some effort is made to achieve it, such as winning the lottery. Some behavior (not much energy) is exerted on it.

d) Weak Whim—Fulfilling the want is of little importance, e.g., wanting to wear one or another piece of clothing.

e) Double Bind—A want accompanied by sabotaging or ineffective behaviors, e.g., wanting to lose weight while overeating.

f) Reluctant Passive Acceptance—Learning to accept what is inevitable, e.g., acceptance of a disease or handicap.

g) Non-desired Active Acceptance—Accepting a consequence as an unfortunate side effect of a desired behavior, e.g., the battered woman who wants to visit her father accepts the possibility that she will be abused. The result is tied to a clear want. She accepts the undesired outcome because it is tied to a desirable want.

h) Fantasy Dream—A want that is seen as unattainable. Wanting to have a family like the "Brady Bunch" when there is overwhelming evidence that this is out of the question.

25. BUFFALO BRIDLE

Weinberg (1985) describes the importance of wants in his insight about how to motivate buffaloes to do what you want them to do. It is not something that is done—it is something that is known, it is a fact of knowledge. He states that you can get a buffalo to go wherever you want it to go . . . if it wants to go there.

The same is true of human beings. The mental picture, the want, the image of quality which is need-satisfying is the motivator of all behavior. A parent, teacher, policeman, dictator, or government can provide rewards, punishments, and a wide range of stimuli in order to motivate people's behavior. The bottom line is that human beings choose to change if the input (stimuli) they get from the outside world is need-fulfilling.

Some people choose to die rather than change their behavior. History is filled with stories of martyrs who refused to denounce their religion and thus were tortured and killed. In wartime, many soldiers and members of the resistance refuse to give vital information to the enemy and choose to keep a secret only to suffer a painful ordeal culminating in death. In short, we choose to do what meets the mental picture of what we want. In your family or at work, have you ever tried to force a person to do something that he/she did not want to do? How effective were your efforts?

26. OUT-OF-BALANCE SCALES

This metaphor refers to the discrepancy between what we want and what we perceive we are getting at a given moment. When we get what we want and our need is thereby fulfilled, we exist in a state of homeostasis—our scales are in balance. For example, when someone is hungry, the scale is out of balance. Behavior is chosen in order to put the scale back in balance. In fact, all behavior is designed to balance or keep in balance our mental scales.

27. CHRYSLER DEALERSHIP

There was a happily married man who owned a very successful Chrysler automobile dealership. When the American public began to buy foreign cars, his business gradually failed. Finally, he lost everything. Even his marriage broke up and he felt totally out of control.

Then, late one afternoon after a meeting with his creditors and banker, he decided to walk to the end of the pier at the ocean and keep walking. After all, things couldn't get worse. As he pondered his fate, staring into the water, he noticed a bottle floating at the bottom of the pier. It had an unusual shape and his curiosity was aroused. The bottle

floated toward the shore and the man followed it. He picked
it up and uncorked it. Immediately, a genie appeared and
told him he could have one wish—whatever he wanted. He
was so happy he blurted out, "I want a foreign car dealership
in a large city." Zap! His wish was fulfilled. He instantly
stood before his own showroom—a Chrysler dealership in
Tokyo.

How important it is to be specific in deciding what we
want. When setting a goal, be sure to make it as precise,
concrete, and complete as you can.

28. MENTAL GOLF GAME

George Hall, an Air Force officer, was a prisoner of war
in Vietnam for seven years. An avid golfer, he played 18
holes of golf every day in his mind. According to Ty Boyd
(1990), he visualized each stroke in detail. His game required
a mental commitment lasting all day. Shortly after returning
home, he played in the New Orleans Open. His score? 76.

The power of a want coupled with the effort to make this
want a reality can have an effect that is profound and far-
reaching. Anyone picturing, imagining, and visualizing the
goal or the want not only influences the outcome of future
behaviors, but also increases the skill required in fulfilling
the want. What behaviors can you choose to get what you
want today?

29. TOW-TRUCK DRIVER'S DREAM AND INSURANCE ADJUSTER'S NIGHTMARE

There was a news report about a fifty-car fender-bender accident on an expressway. The reporter described it as a "tow-truck driver's dream and an insurance adjuster's nightmare." The reason it was a dream (pleasure) for one person and a nightmare (pain) for the other person is that it was want- and need-fulfilling for a tow-truck driver, but the insurance adjuster would face an endless amount of paperwork, details, and added headaches. The element (cause) that determines whether an event is a dream or a nightmare is not the external circumstance, but the internal needs, wants, and scales.

30. FOUR-MINUTE MILE

Our expectations of others do not *cause* them to perform well or poorly and we cannot force others to do anything. But it would be inaccurate to say that we cannot *influence* others. Anyone who is seen by another person as personally important can have some influence on the latter's decisions and behavior. Roger Bannister once said that his coach so believed in his ability to break the four-minute barrier that he was enabled to accomplish this wondrous feat because he "did not want to disappoint" his coach.

31. SKYLINE OF THE CITY

When most people look at the skyline of the city, they see buildings of varying heights. So, too, when many people look at their wants, some are "higher" than others, i.e., more important. They are capable of putting them in priority. But other people viewing their skyline of wants see a series of wants indistinguishable in size.

An example of such a person is a substance abuser or person of any age who is the child of an alcoholic. They have often put contrary pictures in their albums. If children are praised one day for a certain behavior and condemned the next day for the same behavior by an alcoholic parent, they will eventually put contradictory pictures in their albums. They will also choose inconsistent behaviors and have an inadequate sense of what helps them and what doesn't help them. Their experience has taught them to perceive one behavior as being effective at one time and totally ineffective at another time.

Thus the therapist must spend extra time and effort helping such clients define their wants and develop evaluation skills. So, too, a parent who spends time helping a child to clarify wants provides a service for the child that pays big dividends later.

32.   THREE FROGS ON A LEAF

The following riddle is posed: Three frogs were sitting on a leaf. Two decided to jump. How many are left? Answer: Three. It is not enough to decide to jump. Although it is important to define clearly what we want, it is also necessary to take action, to behave in some manner. Intentions need to be translated into effective action. The behavioral system provides the limbs and vehicle for such a delivery system.

5

Metaphors for Behavior

The behavioral system is the delivery method by which we fulfill our needs, get what we want, and put our scales back in balance. Thus, all behavior has a purpose and though one person's actions might seem to others, at times, to be aimless, they nevertheless make sense to the person selecting them. Most behaviors are generated from within and are not caused or forced by external stimuli but by early childhood conflicts or by unconscious drives beyond our control. Behaviors are generated when people perceive that they do not have what they want. A signal is sent to the behavioral system and Total Behavior is set in motion.

The words "Total Behavior" are used to illustrate that all behaviors are made up of four elements: Doing or Acting, Thinking, Feeling, and Physiology. These are like the four wheels of a car, the front two being acting and thinking.

They steer the car, i.e., we have more direct control over these than over feelings or physiology. Though all behavior is composed of all four elements, still, when human behavior is described, we usually identify it by its most obvious component, e.g., walking, depressing, backaching, etc. Ironically, the most easily changed component is the part we are least aware of, the acting element.

Though we can become aware of what we are doing, we are most aware of our feelings and our thinking. Furthermore, a teacher, counselor, therapist, supervisor, or parent can reach out and attempt to help people change, but cannot force them. No matter how influential we are with others, we cannot truly "force" their choice.

33. HANDS AND FEET

The behavioral system is the delivery method for the Needs, Picture Album, and Out-of-Balance Scales. This metaphor is used in conjunction with "Three Frogs." After people decide they want something that they don't currently have, a signal is sent to the behavior system which attempts to put the scale in balance. The behavioral system provides hands and feet for the choice.

34. BEHAVIORAL CAR

Another way to think of the behavioral system is with the analogy of a car. This metaphor seems to explain the deceptively simple notion of "Total Behavior." This analogy is explained elsewhere (Glasser, 1986a, 1988b; Floyd, 1987) and summarized below.

a) Just as the car is made up of four wheels, so, too, behavior is made up of four inseparable components: acting, thinking, feeling, physiology. When the car moves, all four wheels move.

b) The movement of any one wheel of the car cannot be separated from the movement of the other wheels of the entire car. Thus, when a person acts, the other components accompany the deed. When a baseball player swings a bat, the acting does not occur in isolation. Accompanying it is thinking, feeling, and physiology. Also, when a person is "depressing" there are concomitant elements of doing, thinking, and physiology.

c) The total behavior is chosen as a unit, and so no one explicitly chooses to be depressed. The feeling wheel of the car does not move in isolation from the others. The choice is a global or total selection. When choosing a total behavior, we often identify it by the most observable component.

35. DANCING

It is important to dream about the future, to build practical and usable castles in the air. To wish for a better life is praiseworthy, yet it is not enough. There is a saying: "Bloom where you are planted." In other words, start where you are with choices to do whatever you do to the best of your ability. Only then can the dreams become realities and the castles have foundations. Bear Bryant put in another way: "Dance with the one that brung ya!"

36. STEALING A CAMERA

The user of Reality Therapy attempts to help people make better choices. In fact, the notion of "choice" lies at the basis of all human behavior. We choose how to live our lives. Nevertheless, many people do not *feel* as if they have choices. They don't perceive that they can select option A or option B. By using the principles described in this book, it will not only help people make better choices, as stated above, but you will help them perceive that they have many solutions open to them.

In working with female offenders for three years, I learned that they frequently did not perceive that many choices were available. One such client walked into a store and saw a camera on the counter. Only one choice appeared practical at that moment: steal the camera. This choice is available to many people. Yet the vast majority of customers perceive more than one choice, such as: paying for the camera by credit card, check, or by cash; returning at a later date to purchase the camera; not purchasing any camera; or making a layaway arrangement. There might even be other options that are perceived by the reader. In applying the principles of Reality Therapy to persons seeing only one choice, we help them see choices other than "stealing the camera."

37. KATHARINE AND DARRYL: CHOICES

Movie mogul Darryl Zanuck once sent a script to Katharine Hepburn. She felt it was beneath her talent and skill to play the part he ascribed to her. She wrote him three letters similar to those below (Boyd, 1990):

1. *Darryl dear,*
   It will be a year before I can read the script. Thank
   you so much for thinking of me.

                                    Love,
                                    Katharine

She thought about this and wrote the second letter.

2. *Darryl,*
   Offended by the script.

                                    Katharine

She thought some more.

3. *D,*
   Go to hell.

                                    K.

The next day she put all three letters in an envelope with a fourth note:
"Take your choice."
You are invited to make your own applications to human choice, perceptions, and styles of communication.

38. FALLING JET

Occasionally the media carry a story about an airplane that loses its engines. The passengers, having a need for survival which is seriously threatened, quickly search their behavioral systems—their suitcases of behavior—and find there are few effective doing or thinking behaviors that can be found. So behaviors that are primarily feeling behaviors are selected; first worry, then fear, and then panic. All behaviors, even our feelings, have a purpose; they are attempts to get us what we want—in this case survival. In your day-to-day life, do you act worried, fearful, or even panic-stricken? Is there another behavior you could choose?

39. BEHAVIORAL SUITCASE HANDLE

The suitcase is used to further explain and emphasize the importance of Total Behavior and carries it further by suggesting how behavior is changed. In the suitcase is contained four levels of behavior. At the top is acting. Below this level are thinking, feeling, and physiology. The handle is at the top of the suitcase, and when the suitcase is transported, it is carried by the most "grabbable" part—the handle. So, too, when a person seeks to change total behavior it is important to change the most easily changed element—the acting component.

For when it is lifted, i.e., changed, all behavior follows and is also changed. Thus, it is helpful to discuss all four levels (or wheels of the car) with clients, children, or employees. Thinking, feeling, then physiology should be discussed. But it is *most* useful to emphasize changing the acting component. In this way, we lift the suitcase in the easiest manner.

40. WAVING YOUR ARMS

It is difficult to directly change what you think and feel and your physiology. It is easier to change what you do. And when you change what you do, as when you lift the handle of the suitcase, you change all components of the behavior. A simple exercise illustrates the point.

Close your eyes and for ten seconds, try to change your physiology, more specifically your digestion or your blood pressure. It's very difficult to directly accomplish this. Next, close your eyes again for ten seconds and change your feelings to pleasant feelings. Finally, do the same with your thoughts. Close your eyes and change your thoughts to happy thoughts. More likely, you did not show very much change to an observer. Now do this: Sit with both feet flat on the floor and raise your arms in the air. Swing them around as you stamp your feet, shouting "Hooray!" in a loud voice. (The equivalent in Japanese is "Eh, eh, oh!")

You undoubtedly changed your entire behavior. For an instant, you changed your tendons, muscles, etc. You changed your feelings and thoughts for a few seconds. And you accomplished this by changing your actions. It is clear that to change how you act results in a change of Total Behavior. What application can you make to your life today? When you feel depressed, what do you do? What *can* you do?

41. THE ALCHEMIST AND THE HIPPOPOTAMUS

The story is told by Weinberg (1985) about the king who commissioned his alchemist to discover the magic formula for turning lead into gold. In order to get the result he wanted from the alchemist, he added that the formula must work or the alchemist could be executed.

After a while the alchemist returned to the king with a very lengthy and complicated formula. He said that only the king could use it and that it definitely would work . . . on one condition. While the king uttered the formula he must not think of a hippopotamus. Needless to say, the chemist enjoyed a long life. The harder the king tried not to think of the hippo, the more he thought of it, with the result that the metal was unchanged.

It is very difficult to control and change our thoughts directly. Such a change can be made at times, but it is far easier to change what we do and thereby change our thoughts (Waving Your Arms).

42. BLUE SUIT

This metaphor illustrates the same point made by "The Alchemist and the Hippopotamus." Since blue is my favorite color, I frequently wear blue suits at my training seminars. I ask the participants to look at me and not to think about the color blue. It is next to impossible to refrain from such thoughts. In order to avoid thinking about the color blue, it is more effective to take action, to look at something else or to get involved in another activity.

43. LOOSE RUBBER BANDS
AND THE CHAIN OF BEHAVIOR

It is often said that feelings and thinking do not change at the same speed as the acting component. Thus, an employee might change the acting wheel by treating a coworker more cordially. Yet *feelings* of coldness, resentment, and anger might remain for a while and change only after a long period of time, as could some very negative thoughts about that worker.

Similarly, when a person wakes up and "pretends" to be alert and enthusiastic by singing in the shower, there is a time lag between the change in the acting and the change in the feeling and thinking. In like manner, depressed people rarely feel instantly better when they convert their passive acting component to a more energetic schedule.

At first glance, these facts seem to negate the concept of Total Behavior. In fact, they do not serve as a denial of total behavior, but illustrate still another aspect of it. It is true that when the acting component is changed, the feeling component often changes later. It is as if you pull on one end of a rubber band or a chain. After a while, depending on the length and flexibility of the rubber band and the length of or number of links in the chain, the rest of the rubber band or chain is also pulled along.

The explanation lies in the fact that these analogies seem to describe not one total behavior but more than one. The person who sings in the shower while still tired has generated a total behavior. When he/she reports feelings of energy and wakefulness, perhaps seconds or moments later, he/she is comparing the acting component of Total Behavior with the feeling component of Total Behavior and so there is a time lag between "doing better" and "feeling better."

The important theoretical explanation is that we are talking about two total behaviors and comparing the acting component of the preceding behavior with the feeling component of the subsequent behavior.

The practical aspect of the analogy or metaphor is that we need to realize that when we change what we do, we will eventually change our feelings, our attitudes, and even our lifestyles. Can you think of two or three practical applications of these principles in your life?

44. SCULPTOR MOLDING CLAY

This metaphor illustrates that all behavior has a purpose: to control, maneuver, and mold the external world to match the inner wants. A sculptor molds, shapes, and forms the clay to match a set of inner pictures or wants. Michelangelo once stated that contained in the marble was a statue, and his work was designed to liberate the imprisoned figure. Actually, the statue was in the artist's mind, an image, a want. The behavior of chiseling and shaving the marble served the purpose of getting the world—the marble—to match the inner wants of the artist.

We are all artists who attempt to mold our environment to match our inner pictures. Thus, there is a purpose behind our behavior. Sometimes this behavior is characterized by positive symptoms and sometimes by negative ones, i.e., it is often effective and often ineffective. Do you occasionally have a clear picture of what you want but choose totally ineffective behaviors for getting it?

45. LOOSE CHANGE IN POCKET

Did you ever listen to a speaker or talk to a friend who continually jiggled pocket change while talking to you? You were very much aware of this "acting" behavior. The "jiggler" was unaware of this component of total behavior but was very much aware of feelings and thoughts. Perhaps the speaker was concentrating on the speech or feeling anxious about the conversation. In any case, we are less aware of our own feelings and thoughts. However, other people are more aware of the component of behavior that is externalized—the acting part.

46. LIGHTS ON A DASHBOARD OF CAR

Feelings are important in the use of Reality Therapy. They are an integral part of the behavioral system and can be discussed directly, but they are not the causes of other behaviors. Rather, they are like the lights on the dashboard of the car. When they are lit, something in the car needs attention. They do not cause the car to overheat, to lose power, or to run out of gasoline; therefore, it is not enough to merely talk about them, it is necessary to get to the root of the problem. Behind the feeling lights is the system of wants, needs, perceptions, and other behaviors that should be examined. What do your feelings tell you when you feel depressed, angry, guilty, ashamed, resentful?

47. FIFTY-FOOT ROPE

It was said earlier that behavior is a choice. If it is a choice, we cannot force others to do what we think is good for them. Too much absorption with results rather than the *process* for attaining results will lessen the value of the result. The "fifty-foot rope," "lowering the bridge," "going fishing," and the "football coach" touch on this principle.

We can extend a hand, but we cannot coerce someone to take it. Even the person drowning fifty feet from shore has three choices when we throw him a rope: a) to take the rope and be pulled to safety; b) to refuse the rope and try to swim to shore alone; or c) to drown.

A counselor, parent, or supervisor needs to know how to throw ropes and should have a supply of adequate ropes. It is not helpful to throw a twenty-six foot rope and tell the swimmer, "You ought to be grateful, I went more than half way with you."

But even the most skilled user of Reality Therapy cannot push the rope to the person or effectively demand that the drowning swimmer take it. And so, with less life-threatening behaviors, it is important to recognize that people are responsible for their choices and if they choose not to be helped, we still have made every effort to extend ourselves to them. Have *you* ever refused to accept a helping hand when you needed one? Why?

48. GETTING EVEN

As creatures who are social, i.e., designed by nature to interact with each other, we can help others or hurt them by choices. The noblest of our behaviors is to serve others, be altruistic, and reach out to our fellow human beings.

And so, striking back is hardly the highest ethical and moral standard by which we can choose to live. An anonymous quote I once heard was, "Don't get even with anyone unless that person has done you a good turn."

49. LOWERING THE WATER
OR RAISING THE BRIDGE

Many clients hope for something outside them to change. Adolescents want their parents off their backs. A spouse wishes the other spouse would act, think, or feel differently. Management wants labor to change and labor hopes that management will change. It is very difficult to lower the water. It is much easier to raise the bridge. Successful communication focuses on the person who is present rather than on "them."

50. GOING FISHING

My father loved to go fishing. Once when he came home empty-handed, my mother asked him how he did that day. He replied, "Great!" She asked, "How many did you catch?" "None," he said. She asked, "How could you say 'great' if you caught nothing?" His insightful answer was, "My job is to fish. It's the fishes' job to bite. If they don't bite, it's not my fault." He refused to take responsibility for anyone's behavior except his own. How do you feel about your *efforts* when they don't produce the desired results? Could you choose to feel at least somewhat satisfied that you made your best effort?

It is important for us to take responsibility for our own behavior, to extend help, and, most importantly, to recognize that we cannot control others. This analogy and the next one can easily be taught to clients, children, and employees.

51. FOOTBALL COACH

Tom Landry, former coach of the Dallas Cowboys, once said that his job is to teach the players to run, kick, pass, catch, block, and tackle, and "the score takes care of itself." Too much attention to outcome results in less attention to process, thereby diminishing the outcome. Behavior that can be controlled is the focus of effective therapy.

52. RODIN'S *THINKER*

This analogy illustrates the point discussed earlier, that behavior is identified by the most obvious element. The statue is that of a man sitting with his arm on his chin and a pensive expression on his face. It is not called *The Sitter.* Rodin called it *The Thinker* because of the most important behavior which he was trying to portray.

53. TAKE A HIKE

In his book *Control Theory* (1986), William Glasser states that parents can do things *for* their children, *to* their children, or *with* their children. He suggests that the most effective interaction of these three is to do things *with* them. The admonition to spend time with children can be extended to any human relationship. In counseling families or couples, I have found it useful to first examine what pains them and how they communicate with each other. This is done by direct questioning and by observing how they talk during the counseling sessions. But it is not enough and indeed often fruitless to work exclusively on improving communication. It is more effective to discuss how they spend their time together and to make plans to improve this time so that it can qualify as genuine relationship-building time or what Ford (1979, 1988) has called "quality time."

The foundation of strong relationships is time spent together which has several characteristics (Wubbolding, 1988).

1. Effortful: The activity requires expenditure of energy, as in playing a game, etc.

2. Valued: Whatever is done together must be important to each other. If going to a concert is repulsive to one person, the activity will not enhance the relationship.

3. Aware: The participants must at least be aware of the other person, if not need him/her. The above three activities exclude watching TV as quality time. There is little growth in a relationship if television-watching is the extent of the time spent together. Nevertheless, for some people an hour in front of the TV might be more time than they have recently spent together and thus might represent an improvement in the quality of the relationship.

Ford (1988) denies that such activities as fishing together build a relationship. He states: "Fishing isn't quality time *unless there is some interaction.*" I disagree with this position, and take the stance that any time together where two persons are aware of each other, even if they are silent, has a salutary effect on the relationship.

4. Repeated: If the relationship is to flourish or even improve, the behavior must be repeated on a regular basis. Going camping once a year will not sustain a family or a couple.

5. Limited in length of time: The activity need not be lengthy. A few minutes a day is sufficient. Ford suggests that fifteen minutes a day will help a couple change their relationship in a matter of weeks.

6. Enjoyable: The activity should be enjoyable or at least not agony for all parties. If walking, exercising, working, or playing a game together is enjoyable, there is a high likelihood that it will continue. If it

is not need-satisfying, the participants will rapidly become *former* participants.

7. Noncritical: The time spent together should be free of any demeaning comments or put-downs of any of the other person's behaviors. This is always difficult if there is tension between two people, for there is a tendency to put blame on the other person and so biting one's lip can be useful at times.

8. Nonargumentative: Not only is criticism not useful during this mutual activity, but even intellectual arguments and controversies should be avoided. These cannot and should not be totally shunned at other times. *But during this time* they should be avoided. It is better to be silent than to argue during these few precious moments.

9. Past failures avoided: Talk of past misery and failures should be avoided like the plague. Such conversation only serves to arouse pain and make the time repulsive to one or both parties.

10. WDEP discussed: If an activity such as walking allows for talking, it should center on "Radio Station WDEP." It is most useful to emphasize the "D"—Doing. Discussing what happened during the day without making judgments on it, as in the metaphor "Beowulf," is tame and noncontroversial. It also has a calming effect on upset people. It increases their sense of self-esteem in that they feel appreciated for what they do without feeling they "ought" to do and be other than they are.

One of the most valuable activities is to take walks together. It sounds simplistic but it is not. The Danish philosopher/theologian Kierkegaard once said, "There is no problem too great that cannot be solved by walking." And so in counseling busy and harried couples I often ask them to spend fifteen minutes a day walking together. It is realistic because it can generally be done close to home, and it requires little preparation and no special clothing. It is also quite inexpensive. After helping a couple make such a plan, a woman facetiously remarked to me, "We come a long distance to see you, pay you a good fee, commit ourselves to this process, and you tell us to take a hike." We all laughed heartily. I replied, "See, you're already having fun together. Next you'll need to have fun without me being around." I suggest that you ask yourselves about your own "quality time." How much do you have with your spouse, children, or other people close to you? What is your plan for increasing it?

54. TOILET PAPER HUNG BACKWARD

The purpose of all behavior is to gain better control. Sometimes even (especially?) in marriage one person tries to control or change the other. Yet the enlightened person who has tried to change the marriage partner quickly comes to realize after approximately one day of marriage that such efforts are doomed to failure. Energy expended to change another person, to *cause* him/her to behave differently, rarely works and most often leads to frustration for the person trying to force the change.

In other words, if someone hangs the toilet paper backward *before* marriage, he/she will hang it backward after the wedding ceremony is completed.

(Please note: Some readers fully understand this metaphor. If you don't understand it, be assured you are among those who hang it backward!)

55. PLAYING BASEBALL

In learning and applying the principles of Reality Therapy, it is important to focus attention on process rather than outcome. This means that, paradoxically, the result will be more desirable if the behaviors which produce the hoped-for result receive more attention than the result itself.

The baseball player concentrates on keeping his/her eye on the ball, stepping into the pitch, etc. If too much concentration is given to outcome, e.g., the ball going over the fence, the batter will take his eye off the ball and the result will be "a swing and a miss." The overall event is as follows: 1) determination of goal or result; 2) concentration on process (behaviors aimed at the result); 3) need, satisfaction, or enjoyment of the result.

6

Metaphors for Perception and Perceived World

Part of our mental mechanism is a storehouse of perceptions. Glasser (1988) has referred to this as the "all we know world." It contains memories of all our experiences, pleasant and unpleasant, desirable and undesirable. It contains recollections of people, places, events, ideas, etc. A small part of it is our collection of wants or the "all we want world," all the images which have high quality for us.

These images or perceptions are filtered through at least two lenses. In the first lens, or lower level of perception, we merely label the experience, identify it, recognize it. In the second level, we make a judgment about the experience. We approve, disapprove, put a plus, minus, or neutral value on the incoming perception. These perceptions are unique to each individual and give meaning to the external world.

56. FILE CABINET

The perceived world or "all we know world" contains images and memories of everything we have experienced. It is like a huge file cabinet filled with folders. Some are important and some are kept only because we have not made the decision to discard them. Since we don't refer to them on a regular basis, they are kept in a rarely used drawer. Other files are more habitually opened and perused in detail. The latter are wants. If we want information and don't have it, we approach the file cabinet to seek out the desired folder. To mix a metaphor, our scale is now in balance again.

As with all metaphors, the reader is invited to extend this metaphor and discover other nuances in it and possibilities for it.

57. BOSTON TREES IN FALL

When the British writer Matthew Arnold visited Boston for the first time in the fall, he asked a friend, "I say, are your trees infected with a disease?" He had never seen the fall foliage of New England and had no experience to shape his perceptions, except what he had learned up to that point. His perception of them as diseased was based on his experience of the foliage in England, which apparently was quite different. This example clearly illustrates how our perceptions are congruent with the experience we have had. If you want to change your viewpoint, it is first necessary to change your actions or to gain a new experience.

58.   TWO FILTERS

The perceptual system contains two lenses, or two filters, through which is screened the incoming energy from the external world. One is called the "Total Knowledge Filter" and one is the "Valuing Filter." The former is also described as low-level perception. At this level we simply recognize the world around us and label the perception without attaching a significant value to it. We make few, if any, judgments about the perception.

Some perceptions proceed through the valuing filter and emerge with a positive, negative, or neutral value. This filter is a reflection of the wants or the mental picture album. What is desirable is seen to have a positive value. What is undesirable is seen to have a negative value and some perceptions receive the neutral value of indifference.

The role of the helper is often to help lower the level of perception. When people are upset, our role is to help them settle down and relax. On the other hand, sometimes it is advantageous to help clients raise their levels of perception. When a person is overly comfortable with a problem, it is useful, through the use of good Reality Therapy skills, to help him/her begin to place a value on his/her own behavior. For example, the family of an alcoholic would often do well to lower their levels of perception toward the alcoholic person. On the other hand, the substance abuser would do well to raise the level of perception by putting a *very* negative value on the current behavior. What perception of people or of their behavior would you like to change?

59. COMFORT THE AFFLICTED

Some people see the world around them from a very high level of perception. Every event is a major crisis which requires a pro or con judgment. A favorable or unfavorable sentence is passed. As stated above, some people would do well to lower their level of perception and accept whatever cannot be changed. A counselor can help them settle down and relax. Such a helper "comforts the afflicted."

However, the reverse is often true, also. Some people are apathetic, lackadaisical, and overly laid-back about occurrences that bother others. Some employees fail to see the need for promptness, hard work, or even honesty. The counselor or supervisor in this case needs to help them feel some discomfort, some stress, or an out-of-balance scale. Consequently, it is important not only to comfort the afflicted, but in this case to "afflict the comfortable."

60. FAVORITE CHAIR

This metaphor further illustrates the two levels of perception. When participants enter a room for a training session, they usually notice that there are chairs in the room. This observation is probably not accompanied by enthusiastic feelings about the chairs, nor do they put a high negative value on the chairs. They simply perceive them as chairs without making intensive favorable or unfavorable judgments.

But if someone owns a chair that is called "my favorite chair," it is seen from a level of perception where a very positive value is imposed. It is not an object about which no judgment is made. It is a chair that is more than merely recognized by the observer.

On the contrary, a tour of the state penitentiary could reveal a chair that often elicits very negative judgments. The electric chair is not merely recognized as a chair without a value imposed on it. Rather, an intense negative value is placed upon it. As the perception passes through the high-level filter, it receives an intensely negative value.

61. THE UMPIRE

The perceptual system is so important that it can be called an Umpire. In a sense, an umpire creates the reality. The story is told about a baseball pitcher who became impatient with a head umpire who called the pitches too slowly to please the pitcher. About halfway through a game, as the umpire was deliberating about a pitch, the hurler impatiently shouted, "Well, what is it, a ball or a strike?" The umpire replied, "It ain't nothin' 'til I calls it somethin'." Our perceptions are our umpires; they create the reality. Herbert Spencer once said, "It is the mind that makes good or ill, that makes wretch or happy, rich or poor." In a similar vein, Hamlet states that "There is nothing good or bad, but thinking makes it so."

62. WARM ROOM/COLD ROOM

The reader is invited to use the analogy of the umpire to explain this metaphor. Is the room too warm, too cold, just right? Why? Can you accept others' perceptions which are quite different from yours?

63. GROUCHO MARX

The joke is told about the wife of Groucho, who comes home to find him in bed with another woman. Groucho says, "Who are you gonna believe, me or your eyes?" Undoubtedly she will believe the perception received through her eyes as it seems to be more reliable than what she could hear at the moment. Some perceptions are more impressive than others. What many people see is more firmly imprinted in our consciousness than mere words.

Similarly, the medium of television made the horrors of war more tangible during the Vietnam War and served to sway public opinion. For the first time in history, masses of people saw war as it was happening on the front line. These perceptions were valid, lasting, and painful. They created widespread out-of-balance scales among thousands of people who then chose to act in a variety of ways. Also, we don't make total or perfect contact with the world that is external to us. We know and incorporate only what is filtered through our perceptual system.

64. PIG AND COW

The story is told about a man who was driving on a winding country road. It was a warm summer day and the motorists had their windows open. He started around a bend and another car came from the opposite direction. A woman leaned out of the window of her car and shouted "Pig!" In a fleeting second he felt angry that he was unjustly accused of being a chauvinist. He wasn't even "hogging" the road, and so felt this accusation was unwarranted.

Being angry at this name-calling, he returned the perceived insult by shouting "Cow!" (or the equivalent of this word). Then, as he came around his part of the bend, he ran over a pig in the middle of the road. How easy it is to misinterpret others' behavior and give it a meaning they did not intend.

65. TERRIBLE WINTER

Several years ago when we had a very mild and snow-free winter, a friend knocked on my door and said that his car had broken down about a mile away. He asked me to drive him to the nearest gas station so he could ask them for help. The owner of the gas station was only too glad to oblige by sending one of his six tow trucks.

Though I thought I knew the answer, I asked him if he had gotten much use from his tow trucks so far that winter. He looked at me with a disgusted expression and snarled, "No, it's been a terrible winter. I wish we had snow, ice, and below-zero weather so I could get some use from those trucks." Weather that fulfilled my wants and needs created a seriously out-of-balance scale for the owner of the six tow trucks.

66. A DOG NAMED "LUCKY"

The importance of perception is seen in the case of an eleven-year-old neutered dog who has only three legs, is blind in one eye, and answers to the name of "Lucky." As Shakespeare said, "There is neither good nor ill, but thinking makes it so." The perception of ourselves can generally be positive when we consider the alternative. To put it another way, "Bad breath is better than no breath."

67.   LUKE AND ZEKE I

According to Weinberg (1985), Luke and Zeke went to the north country to hunt bear. Luke decided to take a walk outside the cabin. As he opened the door to leave, he was surprised to see a bear ready to spring. He immediately ducked, and the bear leapt over his head, through the open door and into the cabin. Luke quickly slammed the door shut and shouted, "Zeke, you take care of this one while I get another one."

Luke tried to turn a bad situation into a good one, though it is doubtful if Zeke agreed. Such reframing might be need-fulfilling for Luke, but Zeke would probably not feel the same kind of relief.

Perceptions differ among people according to the variances in wants. In all relationships, there are conflicts. One spouse sees golf as fun, another as boring. A business partner sees an expenditure as an investment in the future. Another sees it as a waste of money. One school sees its team as number one. Another school sees its own team as the best. Perceptions are unique to each individual. And the working out of relationships means creating overlap and agreement in perceptions.

68.   IT'S ALL HOW YOU LOOK AT IT

Sometimes it helps to change how we see the world around us. Below are listed some references that can help to make life more beautiful:

"The sight of him doubled her over."

"She was bent on seeing him."

"Your face would stop a clock."

"When I looked at you time stood still."

| "You look like the end of a long, hard winter." | "You look like the first breath of spring." |

The helping professions are the true pros when it comes to reframing. In a skit on the *Tonight Show* on May 29, 1990, George Carlin described the psychological damage done to soldiers in war. In the first World War, it was called "shell shock." In World War II, it was "battle fatigue." And many years after the Vietnam War, we have "post-traumatic stress syndrome."

He also described a caricature of reframing: a dump is now a "landfill." Information became "directory assistance." A swamp is now "wetlands." Toilet paper was renamed "bathroom tissue." A house trailer is called a "mobile home."

Sometimes a failure to understand the reframes that others give to words can be disastrous. In my city, a Chinese restaurant opened and was apparently named after a family. It was named Pflem's. It remained in business only a few months.

69.   YOUR GAS AND ELECTRIC BILL

When you receive your gas and electric bill (or any other bill), read it carefully and note whether you receive a discount if you pay early before a specific date. This example illustrates that reframing negative to positive is widely practiced. The above reframe sounds better than prescribing a penalty for late payment.

70. TOM SAWYER WHITEWASHING THE FENCE

One of the best examples of reframing is seen in *Tom Sawyer*. While Tom is whitewashing the fence for his aunt, he is approached by his friend Ben. Tom describes the chore as an opportunity, telling Ben that it isn't every day that a boy gets to whitewash a fence and that he would rather paint the fence than do anything else. Before the end of the day, not only did Ben get his chance to work, but every other kid in town was begging for the opportunity to take Tom's place at the fence. They even paid Tom for this need-fulfilling opportunity. Think of ways this can be used with your family members.

71. REAGAN'S AGE

In the 1984 presidential election, Walter Mondale hinted that Ronald Reagan's age might be a factor for the voter to consider. In one of the debates, Reagan reframed this and put an end to the issue. He stated that age should not be a factor and he intended to keep this issue out of the campaign. He reframed the issue by saying he would not make his opponent's youth and inexperience an issue.

72. "HOT," "TERMINAL"

To maintain a high degree of mental health and feel good, it helps to gain as much experience as possible in as many areas of our lives as possible. For it is this experience that determines how we perceive the world around us. Boyd (1990) provides some excellent illustrations. For example,

what comes into your mind when you read the word "HOT"?
Depending on your experience you might think of

> fire
>
> coffee
>
> pants
>
> water
>
> popular

He says that if you are an electrician you might think of "wire," and if you are a thief you might think of "stolen goods."

Similarly, what do you think of when you read the word "TERMINAL"?

> train station
>
> bus depot
>
> disease
>
> computer
>
> airport

Your experience with the word determines how you look at it, what you see, and what it means to you. Thus, a wide variety of experience helps open viewpoints and perceptions. A pleasant experience with another person, a new place, or a different race or culture creates favorable perceptions of that person, place, race, or culture.

73. HALLEY'S COMET

The following examples of what can happen when one person's effort at communication (behavior or output) is filtered through another person's perceptual system (perceptual filters and input) comes from Ty Boyd (1990).

*A colonel issued the following directive
to his executive officer:*

"Tomorrow evening at approximately 2000 hours, Halley's Comet will be visible in this area, an event which occurs only once every seventy-five years. Have the men fall out in the Battalion area in fatigues, and I will explain this rare phenomenon to them. In case of rain, we will not be able to see anything, so assemble the men in the theater and I'll show them films of it."

The executive officer writes to the company commander:
"By order of the colonel, tomorrow at 2000 hours Halley's Comet will appear before the Battalion area. If it rains, call the men out in fatigues and march to the theater where the rare phenomenon will take place, something which occurs only once every seventy-five years."

The company commander to the lieutenant:
"By order of the colonel, in fatigues at 2000 hours tomorrow evening, the phenomenon Halley's Comet will appear in the theater. In case of rain in the Battalion area, the colonel will give another order, something which occurs only once every seventy-five years."

Lieutenant to the sergeant:
"Tomorrow at 2000 hours, the colonel will appear in the theater with Halley's Comet, something that appears every seventy-five years. If it rains, the colonel will order the Comet to hit the Battalion area."

And finally, the sergeant to the squad:
"When it rains tomorrow at 2000 hours, the phenomenal seventy-five-year-old General Halley, accompanied by the colonel, will drive his comet through the Battalion area theater in his fatigues."

7

Metaphors for Environment

The vehicles for applying Reality Therapy and the foundational element in the Cycle of Counseling are referred to as "Environment." It implies a responsibility on the part of the helper to establish an atmosphere that is conducive to change and is safe and friendly, i.e., one which facilitates a free discussion by the client. To effect this, the helper listens attentively, is courteous, determined to work things out, enthusiastic, and firm. A sense of humor is very facilitative of change, as is a creative use of the unexpected. Just as this book contains metaphors for understanding and using Reality Therapy, so, too, in applying the principles, it is helpful to listen for metaphors used by people we deal with. An activity is provided in Chapter 12 which is designed to help the reader identify and respond to the others' metaphors. Focusing on the person rather than on outside forces helps to increase the pace of the counseling or supervising. The reasonable use of consequences is incorporated in that human beings seem to change or maintain a behavior if there is a payoff, either positive or negative.

Above all, the practitioner of the Cycle of Counseling keeps the rules and lives by the standards of his/her profession. Thus dual relations are avoided. Confidentiality is respected, and when there is clear and imminent danger, an intervention is made. Not all these rules would apply if you are using the principles as a parent.

The above guidelines, however, are suggested as positive steps for solidifying a healthy environment. Some behaviors also need to be avoided, such as getting bogged down in excuses, criticizing, or even arguing. Such "logical" persuasions only seem to stiffen the resistance. The final injunction for establishing a friendly environment is to avoid giving up on the person or on the Cycle. Helpers need to cling to the belief that a better life is possible for your clients, children, and yourself.

74. LEG IN THE AIR

Establishing an atmosphere conducive to change provides the basis for the utilization of the procedures which will be described below. In applying the principles of Reality Therapy counseling, at home, in the office, or in the classroom, it is essential for the helper, supervisor, or teacher to be courteous. I encourage you to refrain from dealing with a crisis when you yourself are upset—if you can avoid it. When individuals are seriously stressing themselves or upset, sometimes it is counterproductive to deal with an upset student, employee, or child. A simple, large-group upset, sometimes it is counterproductive to deal with an upset student, employee, or child. A simple, large-group activity which I have used in workshops serves to get this point across. You can use it yourself as you read this book.

The group is asked to sit with their feet flat on the floor. They then raise their right foot three inches off the floor and kick it out three more inches like they are kicking a football. They hold it in this uncomfortable position while the leader counts slowly to fifteen. When the number fourteen is reached, the leader stops and asks them if they could effectively deal with an upset person while they are stressing themselves, while they have a "leg in the air." They always agree that when they themselves feel caught up in their own stress and strain, they should not deal with someone else who is upset.

75. SPRAY CAN

Part of the environment is an attitude of hope in the future of the client—that a better life is possible. The motto and underlying attitude in using reality therapy is characterized by the slogan, "We will work it out." If you were to be given a spray can, I would facetiously suggest that you paint this motto in your office, home, or classroom. Positive graffiti would certainly be different. Can you think of other slogans as affirmations that might be useful to you?

76.   EUNUCH IN THE HAREM

Part of establishing a friendly environment is to look for strengths, to see the bright side. The opposite of this is the person described here.

The eunuch in a harem is capable of three things: He can analyze, criticize, and scrutinize, but cannot make a plan. Do you know anyone who sees only the negative and contributes little?

77.   SMOKE SCREEN

People sometimes seek to avoid talking about their own control systems and instead send up smoke screens which take the form of excuses, discussion of issues beyond their control, past behavior, etc. The counselor, teacher, or parent needs to cut through these smoke screens, focus on the person in front of you, rather than allowing the conversation to wander too far from legitimate counseling material. How can you focus on your own behavior rather than on forces outside over which you have no control?

78.   CONQUERING EVEREST

Sir Edmund Hillary is known for successfully climbing over 29,000 feet in conquering Mount Everest. His party spent less than fifteen minutes on the incredibly cold summit of the mountain. How long did he plan for this event? Nine months.

Now that you are familiar with many ideas in this book,

you can probably formulate at least three useful lessons for yourself. My favorite three are written below. After you have written yours, turn the book upside down and compare yours and mine.

1. _____ .
2. _____ .
3. _____ .

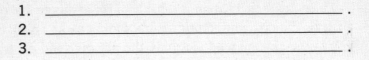

3. We are remembered for our accomplishments but not for our planning.
2. Success can last a short time.
1. Proper planning produces proud performance.

79. CHASING THE RABBIT

When people first learn Reality Therapy, they frequently chase the rabbit. This is the opposite of taking the lead in the counseling session and helping the client develop a sense of direction. A dialogue in which the therapist chases the rabbit might sound like the following. (Such a dialogue also could occur between two friends.)

a. CLIENT: I'm depressed.
b. COUNSELOR: What are you depressed about?
c. CLIENT: My son is on drugs and flunking in school, and I'm upset.
d. COUNSELOR: Does it help to be upset?
e. CLIENT: No. It doesn't help to be upset, but when he comes in drunk at 3:00 A.M. I fly off the handle.

76

f. COUNSELOR: Did you fly off the handle last night?

g. CLIENT: Yes, and my wife got hysterical, too.

h. COUNSELOR: Did it help when your wife got hysterical?

i. CLIENT: No, but she was so upset she couldn't sleep.

j. COUNSELOR: Did you try to help her sleep by talking?

k. CLIENT: No, we sat up and talked about the kids for hours.

l. COUNSELOR: How many hours?

m. CLIENT: Three or four, and we're both tired.

n. COUNSELOR: Would you like me to help you be able to sleep and to relax about this painful problem?

o. CLIENT: I'd like that very much.

p. COUNSELOR: Then I want to ask you some more questions about how you are handling this problem. The areas I'd like to cover are these: What you can reasonably hope for from your son; what you can do that might work; what you can do that won't help; what do you want to gain from these sessions with me, etc.

In this hypothetical but typical exchange, the counselor is not counseling poorly. He/she is making statements that are within the accepted theory and practice of Reality Therapy. But there is no attempt to set an agenda until (n), when the counselor says, "Would you like me to help you be able to sleep and to relax about this painful problem?" It is at that point that the counselor stopped chasing the rabbit; (p) represents even more clearly the need to set a structure, to develop a sense of direction and to *focus*.

It is important to note that "chasing the rabbit" is quite appropriate at times. It can be both necessary and helpful. The point of this metaphor is that a skillful counselor and other users of Reality Therapy know how to do *more* than chase the rabbit. Focusing and structuring are also skills which characterize an advanced level of practice.

80. KEEPING THE HALO STRAIGHT

In maintaining an effective environment, it is of central importance to know and practice a code of ethics if you are a professional helper. Space does not permit an exhaustive discussion of this topic. The reader should consult the works of Woody (1988), Corey (1988), and others as well as the *Journal of Reality Therapy* which contains a regular article on professional and ethical issues. Among the principles which are most important are the following:

a) Advertising should be accurate and in good taste.
b) Dual relationships should be avoided.
c) Within limits, information learned in counseling is kept confidential.
d) Counselor should know how to handle and assess dangerous behavior, i.e., suicidal threats.
e) Appropriate documentation should be utilized.
f) Consultation with other professionals on an ongoing basis should be incorporated.
g) Counselors should know and adhere to the "Standard of Practice" regarding the profession.
h) Counselors should work within the boundaries of their limitations.

The above principles are not exhaustive but are examples of some of the more important standards to be studied in more detail.

81. FIGHTING FIRE WITH FIRE

The idea of fighting fire with fire has always intrigued me. To be successful with this behavior, a person must have more fire than the other person. This might be difficult to achieve and one can never be sure he/she has more fire than the other person. Secondly, it implies resorting to the same kind of destructive tactics that the other person is engaged in. Thirdly, there are definitely losers and possibly no winner in this enterprise.

My suggestion is to fight fire with water. Indeed, when one house is on fire, it is rare for the fire department to burn down the house next door. Rather, they pour water on the burning house in order to extinguish the flames.

So, too, in counseling, parenting, teaching, supervising, negotiating, and in all human relations, it is far better to avoid the power struggle if at all possible. The effective use of the WDEP system does not mean that power struggles can be completely avoided. It *does* mean that they can be lessened. One of the best ways to avoid them is to do the unexpected.

82. FORD'S FUNDAMENTAL FEEDBACK FORMULA

Many years ago, according to Weinberg (1985), Henry Ford was asked to testify before a congressional committee about pending legislation regarding river pollution. He spoke negatively about the detailed rules and regulations that would be required if the legislation was passed. He stated that only two prescriptions were necessary:

1. Any company can dump anything they want into the rivers.
2. Whatever water is removed by companies from the rivers must be removed downstream from whatever they dump into the rivers.

Whether the formula is practical or workable is not the point here. The lesson is that there must be consequences to human behavior. We change or maintain a behavior if it is in our best interest to do so. How many people would keep the traffic laws, pay taxes, or go to work on a cold winter morning if there were no positive (need-fulfilling) or negative (need-denying) consequences? Ford's fundamental feedback formula illustrates that friendship, involvement, and humane treatment are not always sufficient for behavior change. Consequences are also necessary. What consequences could you apply to yourself in order to start or stop a behavior?

83. MICHELANGELO ON CONSEQUENCES

It is stated accurately that consequences must follow from human choices and that we maintain or change our behavior if the consequences are need-fulfilling. Parents regularly impose consequences on children.

Nevertheless, the principle of allowing people to "get

what they deserve" should be applied with temperance. As Michelangelo said in *The Agony and the Ecstasy* (1961), "If we get our just deserts, judgment day will be intolerable for us all."

84. WIND AND SAIL

In handling resistance, Dreikurs (1971) suggests that it is quite efficacious to "take the sail out of their wind." To drop the sail allows the wind to dissipate without counteraction. Without resistance, the wind dissipates. It's been said that "It takes two to argue," and so when one person chooses to agree with another the conflict ceases. This is true in families, among friends, in negotiations, and even between nations.

85. EXCAVATING TROY

Heinrich Schliemann is credited with discovering the ancient city of Troy. His critics repeatedly stated publicly that he was excavating in the wrong place. When the negative comments became vociferous in the Greek newspapers, he was asked to answer them. He refused and simply remarked, "They criticize, I dig." Criticism is generally useless to the plan maker. And so criticism from others is best handled by a positive plan of action and a refusal to answer it. Similarly, self-criticism is best handled by plan making and by repeating one word internally, *"Stop."*

In establishing an environment that is conducive to change, the practitioner of Reality Therapy needs to communicate the opposite of criticism: a belief in the client, and that a better life is possible for them. What will you do to handle, i.e., lessen, your own excuse making?

86. WINSTON CHURCHILL'S ADVICE

When Winston Churchill was an old man, he was asked to give a talk at a high school graduation ceremony. To the surprise of some, he accepted the invitation. When it came time for him to speak, he shuffled up to the microphone and spoke in a weak voice. The following is his entire speech: "Never, never, never give up." He then sat down and the ceremony continued. The ancient warrior could hardly have given better advice to these idealistic young people.

In counseling, we temper this advice by saying, "Don't give up *easily* . . . on the client." We say, "Never give up on the attainment of your own hopes and aspirations," and "Never give up on the principles of Reality Therapy, even if they don't bring about magical cures instantly." The art of helping another person requires time and effort and there is no guarantee of the desired result. People choose their behavior, and with effective counseling, parenting, or supervising, some choose more effective ways of living, but not all. What have you given up on? Do you want to start again?

87. KISSING THE STUDENT

Some teachers shout at students who show unruly behavior, others use negative consequences, while still others employ punitive techniques. Weinberg (1985) describes how one teacher lessened her discipline problems among the boys in her classroom (I have a hunch that these were junior high school students). Sometimes, when one of them was guilty of a minor infraction of a rule she would simply walk up to him and kiss him on the cheek. Needless to say, many students chose to behave rather than suffer such humiliation in front of their friends.

It should be emphasized here that this is presented as an example of a paradoxical technique called positioning and is intended to teach the concept and to do the unexpected. Even if it would work, this author does not endorse it as a technique.

88. MAIN EVENT AND SIDESHOW

In human interactions focus is needed if problems are to be solved, decisions made, or growth attained, yet it is easy to get diverted and side-tracked. Staying with the main event rather than working on interesting but often unhelpful topics is the meaning of focus. Such sideshows include: lengthy discussions of past history, repeated ventilation of negative feelings, complaining about forces beyond our control, bemoaning the unfairness with which people treat us, and others.

The user of the principles of Reality Therapy in school, in home, on the job, or in the counseling center attempts to focus on what can be changed. This does not imply being harsh, cruel, or even abrupt with people. It means that while sideshows might be viewed for a while, the main event receives the most emphasis. This is accomplished by the skillful use of the WDEP system.

89. EXTENDING YOUR HAND

To continue the point above, we can extend a hand to people in need, but we cannot force them to take it. We can set a friendly atmosphere for the client, in the home, at the office or plant, but we cannot force the person to choose responsible behavior. It is important to extend the hand, but also to recognize that some will choose not to extend theirs. How can you extend your hand to someone today? What plan will you make to do this?

8

Metaphors for Direction and Doing

The procedures used in the Cycle of Counseling consist primarily of the WDEP system. This metaphor is explained in Chapter 11. The "W" was also discussed in Chapter 4 under "Picture Album" or "Wants." The "D" stands for Direction and Doing. The practitioner of Reality Therapy discusses the overall direction that the person's behavior is taking them. This quickly leads to a description of specific behaviors. The helper insists that the person be precise in describing exactly what happened. The emphasis is on the acting part of Total Behavior because that is what is most directly under control. We can change the other components of our behavioral system when we change the action part of behavior. This scrutiny of current behavior, as well as perceptions and wants, is followed by an evaluation of their effectiveness and attainability (Chapter 9).

90. YESTERDAY

It is both time-saving and revealing to describe *specific* behaviors that you chose on a *specific* day such as yesterday. I suggest you write a detailed rundown of exactly what happened. This technique is used in conjunction with the next metaphor.

91. TV CAMERA

In describing the events of a *specific* day such as yesterday, it is helpful to ask yourself *specific* and detailed questions, as if to record exactly what happened. In that way, you become a TV camera, as it were. A TV camera does not record generalities—it records specifics: events that happened once and will never happen again in exactly the same way. This variation helps to assess the seriousness of the problem and to formulate a sense of direction. Even more, it serves to help you become aware of the acting part of your total behavior. As in "Loose Change in Pocket," we are least aware of the acting part of the total behavior. The "Yesterday Technique," "TV Camera," and the "Mirror Technique" help you focus on the part of the behavior that you are least aware of but over which you have the most control (cf. "Suitcase Handle").

92. KICKING THE SOFT-DRINK MACHINE

The classroom building in which I teach my graduate counseling classes is located near the street in a suburban neighborhood. In this building, just outside my classroom, is a large soft-drink machine. The junior high and high school students from the area frequently enter the building to get soft drinks from this dispenser.

One evening while I was teaching the "mirror technique" to the students, I heard a loud thumping sound in the hall. I immediately recognized the noise because I had heard it many times before. It was the sound of a frustrated adolescent kicking the machine that refused to surrender a can of soda. I opened the door and the students heard the following conversation between a fourteen-year-old boy and me. In this exchange, I asked the Reality Therapy question that focuses attention on the "acting" aspect of Total Behavior and which is eminently useful in disciplinary situations:

"What are you doing?"

"I'm trying to get a soft drink."

"Yes, but I heard a pounding sound."

"Oh . . . yes . . . I was kicking the machine."

"What's the rule about kicking the machines?"

"Huh?"

"We have a rule about kicking the machines."

"What are you talking about?"

"Our rule about this is, 'No kicking of the machines.' "

The young man's expression was that of total dismay. He looked at me with a friendly but rueful smile, turned around, and walked out of the building, shaking his head as if to say, "Man, is this place weird."

It was indeed a teachable moment for the students. They learned that the use of the mirror technique does not elicit hostility. Rather, it puts responsibility where it belongs, and helps people think differently about their behavior. The event also illustrates how we are more aware of what we want and what we are thinking than what we are doing (the acting aspect of behavior).

The effective user of Reality Therapy knows how to focus on both the wants as well as the purposeful actions designed to fulfill the wants, especially when we are marginally aware of our actions.

93. MIRROR TECHNIQUE

This strategy is based on the principle that it is better to *ask* than to *tell*. When you use these ideas to talk to another person, it is useful to hold a mirror before them so that they can see themselves. Ask them: "What are you doing?" "How are you spending your time?" "What specifically did you do yesterday and did it help?" "Did it work?" "Was it to your best advantage and to the benefit of others?"

This technique provides a bridge between the narration of their current behavior and their evaluation of it. It involves both their discussion of each component of their total behavior (especially the "acting" component) and their evaluation of the effectiveness of specific behaviors.

9

Metaphors for Evaluation

The most important procedure in the Cycle of Counseling is that of Evaluation. Elsewhere (1990a) I have described thirteen kinds of evaluation that are useful in communication with another person. Six are more relevant to the professional counselor and relate to the ethical behavior of the professional counselor. Any change in behavior is accompanied by an evaluation that a previous behavior was not helping or was not helping *enough*. Other forms of evaluation include helping people determine whether their current perceptions are appropriate or advantageous, whether their level of commitment is as high as it could be, and whether their plans fulfill the qualities of good plans.

Frequently, because we are human, we repeat behaviors, even though, at some level of awareness, we know they are not effectively need-fulfilling.

And so the helper attempts to get the person to conduct a searching inventory on the various elements of his/her control system, quality world, behavioral system, and perceptions.

94.   KEYSTONE IN ARCH

The keystone of an arch is its most important stone. If the arch is to remain in place and serve its purpose, the keystone must remain in place and support the other stones. The successful functioning of the structure depends on the keystone. If it is removed, the arch will become merely a pile of rocks. Helping people evaluate the various aspects of their control systems is an absolute prerequisite for any sustained change from a less satisfying to a more need-fulfilling lifestyle.

The most important evaluation statements are summarized here:

a)   Is what you're doing helping you?

b)   Is what you're doing against the rules? (Used in disciplinary situations.)

c)   Is what you want realistic?

d)   Does it help you to perceive the situation as you currently see it?

e)   Is your present commitment for change the best or highest that you are willing to make?

f)   Is the plan which you've made the most effective plan you are capable of formulating?

g)   How am I (the counselor, parent, supervisor) doing in my professional behavior?

This is an evaluation that the helper formulates in reference to this particular conversation as well as his/her overall level of skills.

In summary, the mirror technique combined with evaluation is central to the effective application of the principles of Reality Therapy. If a friendly relationship and a safe atmosphere are the foundation, evaluation provides the keystone.

95. LOST CAR KEYS

Have you ever misplaced your car keys? What is the first behavior you chose? Aggravation, then irritation, anger, and panic, especially if you are in a hurry. Yet, these do not help. The next behavior is to look for the keys. If you cannot find them, do you look again in the same purse, the same pockets, the same spot in the yard where you might have dropped them? If they don't appear after the third or fourth time, do you search again in the same place? Why? The reason is that many of us have an undying belief and hope that repeating useless behavior might work if we try once again. Maybe, just maybe, the keys will miraculously appear when we look in the same place once more!

The solution to this quite unproductive behavior is to ask, "Is this futile behavior helping me?" The next step is to plan to do something different.

96. SPINNING YOUR WHEELS

This analogy represents the same principle as the "Lost Car Keys." In our culture, we frequently use the expression "I was spinning my wheels." This usually means that the same behavior is repeatedly chosen even though it does not work.

97. YELLING AT YOUR KIDS

The principle underlying this metaphor is the same as the "Lost Car Keys" and "Spinning Your Wheels." This one strikes closer to home with many people. They are asked if they "yell at" their kids. Most admit they do, and that it doesn't work. In spite of the fact that yelling doesn't work, it is widely practiced, at least in western civilization.

The irony is that if it worked, one yell would correct the behavior and no parent would need to yell the second time. The very reason we yell at the children is that it does *not* work. As illogical human beings, we seem to relentlessly pursue unevaluated behaviors that are unproductive. And so the procedure of *evaluation* plays a central role in the practice of Reality Therapy.

98. SISYPHUS—NOT A MYTH

In ancient Greek mythology the story is told of a person who is condemned to forever push a rock up a hill only to have it roll down and have to be pushed up again. A frustrating way to spend eternity! Yet it is no secret that many people, as if on a treadmill, continue to repeat the same behavior only marginally aware that it is not working. The "E" of the "WDEP" system helps such a person change ineffective behaviors. As in "Lost Car Keys," an evaluation of the effectiveness of current behavior is useful in order to change and grow.

99. CACTUS ROLLING

William Glasser is fond of telling the story of a man who was walking through a cactus garden in Arizona. Suddenly, to the surprise of bystanders, he tore off his clothes and threw himself into a row of cactus and rolled around in them. The horrified people in the garden were able to extract him from the torturous bed and get him to a hospital where he received proper treatment. He was asked why he did such a senseless thing. He answered, "It seemed like a good idea at the time."

Such outlandish behavior could illustrate many aspects of Reality Therapy: all of human behavior is an attempt to fulfill human needs; people have very diverse perceptions of what is good for them; human beings do, in fact, choose their behavior, etc. The aspect of Reality Therapy I wish to emphasize here is that many people fail to evaluate their choices properly or thoroughly. Central to effective need-fulfillment is the skill in examining the effectiveness of one's behavior, in asking, "Is this choice to my best short-term and long-term advantage and is it congruent with my values?" (cf. "Spinning Wheels"). The cactus victim failed to effectively evaluate the short- and long-term results of his choice. And so the person utilizing Reality Therapy holds the mirror before the other person and asks many questions such as,

"Will this choice get you where you want to go? And is your destination truly helpful to you?"

100. BUCKET IN THE EMPTY WELL

Earl Nightingale once described the person who repeatedly dropped a bucket into an empty well only to draw out . . . an empty bucket. The person did this in spite of the fact that the behavior did not work, was not effective, failed to help anyone, and was a totally futile effort.

The person undoubtedly continued the behavior because no other behavior was seen to be practical. This is true of many people who figuratively drop a bucket into an empty well in many aspects of their lives. A parent I know grounded his son dozens of times in two years even though it did not help and was, in fact, only serving to increase the resentment, anger, and obstinacy of the child.

On the other hand, through the skilled use of the "mirror technique" the person using Reality Therapy facilitates the evaluation of behavior and suggests, "If dropping the bucket in the empty well is not working, let's look for another well."

10

Metaphors for Planning

The culmination of the Cycle of Counseling is a plan of action. "To fail to plan is to plan to fail." Even though a plan might be difficult to attain in every case, still, the user of Reality Therapy principles needs to make plans that can be realistically carried out.

There are two kinds of plans: linear and prescriptive. The linear plan is the usual kind of plan made most of the time. If a person is depressed, a plan is made to get active or get involved with people rather than remaining apathetic and passive. Conversely, a prescriptive plan is a plan to perform the problem behavior. Such a person could plan to be depressed for a short time each day. In carrying out such plans, the person gains better control of the symptom. Any use of paradoxical techniques should include a strict adherence to ethical standards (Wubbolding, 1988), and prescriptive plans should never be employed when dangerous behavior is involved.

Conrad Hilton built a worldwide chain of hotels. He said (1957) that he did it with two main tools: a dream and a plan. People who live the philosophy of Reality Therapy do not wait for events to control them. Rather, they *make* things happen.

101. WINNING THE LOTTERY

Shelby desperately wanted to win the lottery. Each night Shelby prayed for hours to be granted the favor. The prayer was "Let me win the lottery. Please God, you said, 'Ask and you shall receive.' I'm asking with all my energy. I want to hold you to the promise. Let me win the lottery." Shelby prayed nightly for this gift. After about six months Shelby added a question to the entreaty, asking "What do I have to do to win the lottery?" Suddenly there was a loud thunderclap, the room became brightly lit, a cloud opened, and a deep voice from heaven stated, "First you gotta buy a ticket."

It is necessary to have a clear picture of what we want, as did Shelby, but it is not sufficient. A plan is needed to back up the desire. If counselors, therapists, parents, or supervisors can communicate a sense of urgency, a sense of hope, and a sense of belief in the clients, students, or workers, they will more likely realize that it is within their power to take better charge of their lives and to feel better. There are many Shelbys, many people who are in pain and are immobilized, afraid to act, or unaware of what to do. The practitioner of Reality Therapy gets people moving through plan-making and action-taking. If you are a "Shelby," what plans could you make *now* to make your life more satisfying?

102. "CARPE DIEM"

As a college student I wrote this motto above my desk and read it many times each day. In 1989 it became enshrined in the popular culture of America and elsewhere when it was taught by the teacher played by Robin Williams in the movie *Dead Poets' Society*.

It means "seize the day." Use the precious commodity of time to your best advantage. Practitioners of Reality Therapy teach people to make daily plans that can be successful, that are need-fulfilling, that increase self-esteem, that contribute to a person's environment.

This metaphor not only illustrates the need for effective planning in the use of Reality Therapy, it also illustrates the fact that we need to help the people think in ways that are different from past ineffective ways. Often the helper repeatedly tries in vain to induce a person to make plans. It is sometimes more effective to work on the person's behaviors that are primarily thinking behaviors, and to encourage him/her to put less self-defeating, more positive thoughts in his/her mind on a regular basis. Such injunctions as *carpe diem* and other affirmations are useful. How could you "*carpe diem*" more effectively today?

103. TOP OF THE OAK TREE

In his book *See You at the Top*, Zig Ziglar says there are two ways to get to the top of an oak tree. Climb it, or plant an acorn and sit on it. This metaphor points to the importance of planning, of *making* things happen rather than *waiting* for them to happen. No further explanation is required except to ask you to think about three kinds of people who make plans (or who fail to make plans).

1. There are people who *make* things happen.
2. There are people who *watch* things happen.
3. There are people, who, *after* things happen, ask "What happened?"

In using Reality Therapy, the goal is to help people take better command of their own lives and thus to *make* things happen. What could you "make happen" today that will improve your life or the lives of people around you?

104. TEARING DOWN A BRICK WALL

Did you ever try to tear down a brick wall? What is the hardest part of this task? The most strenuous part of this effort is extracting the first brick. After that is accomplished, the rest is easy. So, too, in planning, the most difficult part of any plan is getting started. After some success is seen, it becomes easier to maintain the effort. What first step will you make now to have a better life for yourself or someone else?

105. THOMAS EDISON'S EXPERIMENTS

Thomas Edison tried over 10,000 experiments before he hit on the one that worked. To many people, this would be discouraging. At one point, he was interviewed by a reporter who asked him what it was like to be right where he started after 10,000 tries. He answered that he was not right where he started from. Far from it. He was 10,000 steps ahead of where he had been because he knew 10,000 things that did not work. Like Abraham Lincoln, he failed his way to success.

An effective planner is not consumed with failure. Rather, an ineffective plan is seen as a stepping stone, as a necessary prerequisite to success. Thus, the failed plan is reframed as a leap forward. Discouraged parents need not be overwhelmed when they are trying to help a troubled child; a teacher who has tried and "failed" in his/her efforts to get across to the children need not be flattened by failure. Rather, it is useful to realize that the next plan is the one that will work. What is your next plan for success?

106. TODAY SHOW, TONIGHT SHOW

The plan should be immediate, not remote. One person dealing with procrastination adopted the theme "The Today Show" and "The Tonight Show." It served as a metaphor for immediate action. Whenever she hinted that she would do it later, I would ask, "Is this 'The Today Show'?" She would often respond, "Okay, I got the message. I'll do it now." Once, she said she would make a phone call the next day. I said, "There's the phone on the desk, how about calling now?" She did. She called another city 500 miles away and talked for five minutes!

107. WILLIE MAYS

The great superstar did not give up, but kept planning. The first twenty-six times to the plate he did not get a hit. What if he had given up at that point? Fortunately for millions of fans, he came to bat the twenty-seventh time and the world was given a great gift: the talent of this incomparable athlete. Like Thomas Edison and Abraham Lincoln, he "failed" his way to success.

108. UGLY FACE

There is an African proverb, "If your face is ugly, learn to sing." The point is to capitalize on existing strengths. This proverb allows for much discussion. The reader is invited to consider the many meanings of it.

109. MAGGIE KUHN'S ARTHRITIS

The founder of the Gray Panthers once said, "My arthritis kills me, but if I get involved, I forget it." The statement reflects the power of positive action plans that are need-fulfilling. No one can *promise* less physical pain, but an effective sense of belonging, achievement, enjoyment, and independence can, at times, bring about a better sense of inner control. How will you "get involved" today?

110. LANDING AN AIRPLANE

Imagine yourself on the jetliner as it approaches its destination. It has been a turbulent flight and you are relieved as the pilot announces, "We are beginning our final approach." But he adds, "I will now *try* to land the plane." The turbulence which was previously outside the plane suddenly feels like it is inside your stomach. You turn to the person next to you and ask, "Did he say 'try'? I'd like him to do more than 'try.' I'd like a higher level of commitment."

In the art of helping another human being perform better, grow personally, overcome a problem, or make a decision, the helper needs to elicit a commitment to change from the helpee. So, too, in getting what you want. It is most useful to obtain or at least aim at the highest level possible. In this effort, five levels of commitment can be considered (Wubbolding, 1988):

1. *"I don't want to do anything about the problem."*

   This is the lowest level of commitment and, in fact, is no commitment. The goal of the helper is to encourage the helpee to raise the level to at least the next level. A person who is coerced into counseling by parents, a judge, the school, etc. often exhibits this first level of commitment.

2. *"I want the outcome, but I do not want to make a plan."*

   A person at this level of commitment wants to lose weight, get along better, graduate from school, or get a better job. The attainment of this goal is precluded by the failure to formulate the specific steps to reach it.

3. *"I'll try, I could."*

   This is a weak commitment for the airline pilot. Yet it can be a major step forward for persons who previously expressed levels one and two. Also, cultural differences should be considered here as in all communication. In Japan, for example, "I'll try to do such and

101

such" represents a firm commitment, possibly the fifth level.

4. *"I will do my best."*

Doing one's best represents a fairly high level of commitment. And it seems to be a higher level of commitment than the first three levels. Still, most airline passengers hope for the next level of commitment.

5. *"I will do whatever it takes."*

This statement symbolizes the most that can be humanly expected. It implies a determined, relentless effort that ceases only when the desired result is attained.

Eliciting or making a commitment represents a component of Reality Therapy that serves as the foundation for the use of the Cycle of Counseling and the "WDEP" system. It is part of the "W" and speeds up the process as well as serving as a basis for future growth change. This concept is useful whether you are using the idea with others or as self-improvement techniques.

A word of caution in using the levels of commitment: the five levels should be seen as developmental. They represent stages. For some people, a middle-level "I'll try" is a step forward in their progress. They need not be pushed prematurely to the higher level. The underlying principle is to accept people where they *are* and lead them gently and gradually to a higher level of commitment. Now, pause and examine your own levels of commitment to getting what you want at home, at work, etc.

111. JOURNEY OF A THOUSAND MILES

There is a Chinese proverb that states, "A journey of a thousand miles is begun with one step." This metaphor and the next two, "Steering Wheel on Car" and "Fine-tuning the Dial," illustrate the same point about planning. In making the plan, it is quite helpful to make one small step or to make even a slight change. In the book of cases on Reality Therapy, *What Are You Doing?* (1980), a depressed, suicidal teenager reluctantly planned to keep the drapes open in his room while he continued to seclude himself there on weekends. This was the first step of a long journey to better mental health. What first steps will you choose to take today?

112. STEERING WHEEL ON CAR

If the steering wheel on a car is turned very slightly, it matters little at first—for the first five feet. But when the wheel is kept at even a slight turn for five hundred feet or so, the car will take or make a turn. Such change is more than microscopic, more than merely noticeable, it is major, and can change the total direction of the vehicle. So, too, with a small plan. In what areas of your life do you want to make a change of direction? How will you turn the steering wheel today?

113. FINE-TUNING THE DIAL

When the dial on the radio is not set exactly at the desired station, the program will be garbled at best. It is important to fine-tune the program. So it is with planning. Even a small plan, or a slight change, can make a big difference when repeated.

114. COLUMBO TECHNIQUE

In the TV series "Columbo," the detective was fond of saying to the suspect as he (Columbo) was leaving, "One more thing . . ." Then would follow a blockbuster statement such as, "We have your fingerprints on the weapon."

In helping someone make a plan, it is often helpful to add one more plan. If they are willing, for instance, to spend ten minutes a day with their child, talk about school with the child, and ask the child to help do the dishes, the helper could add, "Just one more thing . . . could you write down what happened; in other words, keep a log so that we can review it next time?"

The purpose of the "Columbo Technique" is to try to increase the success, the effective behaviors of the client, and to increase the likelihood that he/she will follow through on plans.

115. MONKEY ON THE BACK

A metaphor frequently used by management trainers is that of the employee who carries the "monkey on the back" and attempts to give it to the supervisor or manager. It is called "upward delegation." The worker delegates the problem, in a reverse manner, to the boss. The same can happen in client-counselor, parent-child, or other relationships. The person, in effect, says, "Here is the problem. What are you going to do about it?"

In training for human service case-workers and counselors, I have found that they frequently are faced with objections from clients about the fairness of the rules. A case-worker who attempts to be empathetic often goes to the extreme of trying to justify the system, and trying to convince the benefit-recipient of the equity of the new or old rules. The problem has become the counselor's burden. No wonder there is burnout among people in the helping professions.

The goal of the counselor, supervisor, manager, teacher, case-worker, or parent is to take *fewer* monkeys, to help the person solve the problem, or at least live with it and plan better. One thing is certain: If as a counselor, teacher, supervisor, manager, or case-worker you accept every monkey that is offered in a week, by Friday your office will be a zoo.

116. WHO'S GOT THE GOLD?

While it is usually a good idea to be democratic and involve people in making rules, it is sometimes necessary for a parent or another authority figure to make rules and plans for other people. It is idealistic and sometimes quite unrealistic to think that all adolescents are going to agree to an early curfew. Employees may want a policy of "flextime." Students might want to cancel the final exam. Such wants cannot be fulfilled and the authority must make a rule.

It is said that sometimes an authority (usually the parent) should communicate to the parties involved that they are practicing "the golden rule": "Whoever makes the gold makes the rules." This principle is easily abused, used to an excessive degree. Have you ever abused this principle?

117. CHINESE BAMBOO TREE

The "P" of the $\frac{SAMIC^3}{P}$ plan (see page 107) is explained by the analogy of the Chinese Bamboo Tree, the Moso.

Chinese farmers plant the seeds and water the ground. They repeat the watering for five years. During this time, the plant is not visible. It does not even break the soil. In the sixth year, it grows ninety feet in six weeks.

Some plans do not result in the desired payoff for years. Planning is an investment whose visible results are observable only at a later date. And so the "P" stands for a characteristic of the planner, rather than the plan. The person, the client, the manager, the teacher using Reality Therapy needs *perseverance.* What seeds do you need to be planting so that you can reap a plentiful harvest at a later date?

118. TRYING TO STAY AWAKE

Most plans used in counseling are linear plans. These address the problem directly. Thus, if you are awake in the middle of the night, the usual plan is to try to sleep. If a person is filled with worries, the first plan is to attempt to do something about the worries. If someone is anxious about an exam, the plan should be to study for the test.

On the other hand, sometimes linear plans don't work. At times "trying" to sleep does not bring about drowsiness. In fact, it can result in more wakefulness. So, too, fighting worries can sometimes increase them.

And so a paradoxical plan can be used. I often suggest to people to try to stay awake when they cannot fall asleep at night. They should lie in the dark, eyes wide open, and stare at the ceiling. Or, the next time you start to blush, instead of fighting it, try to make it worse.

The use of paradoxical planning fits quite well with Reality Therapy and should be used within ethical guidelines, especially the injunction that no paradoxical plan should be used when destructive behavior is involved. In order to use this technique, the reader should consult the books referred to in the bibliography by Fay (1978), Weeks and L'Abate (1982), Wubbolding (1986), and Belken (1986).

119. INTENTIONAL WALK

A baseball pitcher occasionally walks a batter intentionally. It is a technique that is used to achieve a desired outcome. It is used discreetly and less frequently than direct pitching. Paradoxical techniques are similar. They should be used as an occasional technique.

120. $\frac{SAMIC^3}{P}$

"$\frac{SAMIC^3}{P}$" planning, along with "Radio Station WDEP," are the two most important metaphors contained in this book. They constitute essential components in the practice of Reality Therapy. In $\frac{SAMIC^3}{P}$ planning, each letter stands for a characteristic of an effective plan, and the "C" stands for three characteristics. The "P" refers to the person making the plan.

S = Simple   Keep the plan simple. It should not be so complicated that it cannot be implemented.

A = Attainable   The plan should be realistic. It should be such that it can be done by the client, even though it does not

107

accomplish an ultimate goal. And so, if a student has not taken a book home all year, it is probably unrealistic to expect that a plan to study for two hours every night will be carried out. An initial plan could be to take *one* book home *one* evening.

M = Measurable

Any plan should be specific and exact. An imprecise and vague plan is doomed to failure. As Yogi Berra once said, "If you don't know where you're going, you're sure to end up someplace else." To gain exactness in planning, key questions should be asked: "When will you do it?" "What time?" Anyone making a plane reservation wants to know the exact time of departure. If the travel agent were to say, "The plane will leave sometime this weekend," you would attempt to get more precise information so that you don't sit at the airport from Friday until Sunday waiting for the execution of this imprecise plan.

I = Immediate

The plan should be implemented "ASAP." Good questions for the counselor to ask are, "What will you do today that is different from what you would have done if you had not talked to me today?" "What will you do tonight to turn your life around?"

"What will you do when you leave this office?"

C = Controlled by the Planner	The plan does not depend on what others do. Successful planners make plans that depend *only* on their own resources. Of course, we are all dependent on this to some extent. So this, and the other characteristics of effective plans, should not be carried to extremes. But the plans "to look for a job if someone wakes me in the morning" or "to get along with my brother if he lets me alone" or "to be friendly with my co-worker if she is friendly to me" are not effective plans. The success of these plans is too dependent upon what others do.
C = Consistent	The best plan is repeated on a regular basis or until it is no longer needed. There is a saying that many teachers apply to students who wish to master a subject: "Repetition is the mother of all study." To master a golf swing, it is not enough to practice one hour. To deepen a relationship, it is not enough to spend fifteen minutes together once a month. To overcome depression, it is not enough to get out of bed early one day. To conquer procrastination, it is not enough to make a "to do" list one day. Continued effort is the key to change.

It was said earlier that the plan

should be realistic and it was implied that a one-time plan was acceptable. Such a plan is appropriate at first in the early stage of personal growth, but if lasting therapeutic movement is to occur, the user of Reality Therapy needs to make plans that are repetitious.

C = Committed to   A plan needs to be firm, perhaps written down. A suggestion is that if it is a plan to accomplish something, tell it only to people who will support you. If it is a plan to give up something such as smoking, tell it to everyone. They will help you raise your level of commitment. Other suggestions include writing it down, giving yourself consequences if you fail to follow through or a reward when you do carry it out, etc.

121. STUDYING MATH

After conducting a training session for classroom teachers, one of them reported the following incident: A certain student habitually refused to do his math work in the class. The teacher's behavior frequently gave purpose to his resistance. He would more adamantly refuse in a silent, surly manner.

After hearing about how paradoxical techniques could be used, she applied the principles in a very subtle way. She did not tell him not to study math. Rather, she asked him to write down on three-by-five-inch cards five reasons (one for each day of the week) why he did not want to study math. She also told him to write on the cards how he would communicate to her that he would not study math that day. The cards she collected contained the following information:

1. Because this work is boring here at this school.   Close my book.
2. I don't like geometry.   Put my book on the desk.
3. Because I don't like this school work.   Ask to go out in the hall.
4. I get grouchy.   Put my pen in my desk.
5. I never did like school work.   Say "leave me alone."

Upon a return visit two weeks later, I talked to the teacher, who related that the student had not refused to study one single day! We were both astonished at the change and recognized the value of paradox.

122. READING THE BOOK

Part of the treatment plans which I help clients make is to outline a reading program. Not everyone chooses to follow through with their reading, however. One client returned week after week without having done her "homework." As she was going out the door at the end of the session, I casually remarked, "I don't think you're ready for the reading program. Hold off on that for a while." She returned the next week and we discussed the book, which she had read in its entirety. She would not be restrained by the paradoxical restraint.

123. CARRYING THE TEXTBOOK HOME

A paradox is something that seems to be false but is true. Applied to human behavior, we can, as Fay (1978) suggests, make things better by making them worse. One paradoxical technique is to restrain people from doing what they probably won't do anyway, or to suggest that they continue to perform a behavior they are trying to overcome (prescription). These techniques are usually used to deal with "resistance." I suggest you try one of the paradoxical techniques on yourself first, before using them with others.

In talking to a junior high student who chose not to study, I asked if he could carry one of the books home but not open it. "Even if you get the overwhelming urge to study, fight it off heroically," I said. He smiled and made the plan. The purpose of all behavior is to gain control. Thus, when the student chose to resist studying, he was acting purposefully. Perhaps the student was attempting to gain control of parents, teachers, or even himself. The more the people around him preached, persuaded, or pursued him with "logical" arguments, the more resolute was the defiance. Milton Erickson spoke of "joining the resistance," i.e., using their resistance paradoxically to help them.

124. LUKE AND ZEKE II

Our friends Luke and Zeke were on another hunting trip. Weinberg (1985) describes how one morning, while eating breakfast, there seemed to be an earthquake. The entire cabin was being torn from its moorings. They quickly realized that the earthquake was actually a hungry bear trying to break through the walls to eat them and their food. They began to vacate the cabin quickly when Luke stopped to change his shoes. He took off his hunting boots and began to put on his gym shoes. Zeke was surprised at this and said in a rather panicky tone, "You're never going to outrun the bear just because you wear gym shoes." Luke retorted, "I don't have to outrun the bear. I only have to outrun you!"

Although some would argue that this metaphor illustrates the primacy of the survival need over the belonging need, I include it to illustrate that a plan need not solve every aspect of the problem. Sometimes there is no available ideal plan, no possible plan for resolving the issue, only a plan that addresses the question. But the axiom "to fail to plan is to plan to fail" is relevant. Sometimes it is necessary to make effective plans in order to get to a better one (Thomas Edison's experiments). What is your self-improvement plan for today?

125. "THE SABOTEUR"

In helping clients, students, supervisors, or children formulate plans, it is useful at times to ask them to firm up the plan, to be committed to it, and to pursue it relentlessly. To aid in sealing the commitment, it is often appropriate to ask, "How could you sabotage the plan if you were to choose not to follow through?" If this is done humorously and in a friendly manner, it can strengthen the resolve quite effectively in a reverse maneuver.

For practice purposes there is space provided below for you to write five plans and how you could (but would not) undermine your plans. There is also space for you to write a secondary plan for dealing with the urge to sabotage it. I have included one of my own to help you get started.

PRIMARY PLAN	POSSIBLE SABOTAGE PLAN	SECONDARY PLAN TO GET PAST THE SABOTAGE PLAN
1. Exercise fifteen minutes in the morning.	1. Tell myself "I have plenty of time to do it later today."	1. Tell myself "Do it now."
2.	2.	2.
3.	3.	3.
4.	4.	4.
5.	5.	5.

126. ALICE IN WONDERLAND

It is important to keep planning even when plans do not succeed. To attain the desired result it is frequently necessary to build on what appear to be failures. Lewis Carroll had fifty turn-downs from the publishers before his book *Alice in Wonderland* was accepted by a publisher. Fortunately for the world, he kept planning.

127. POLITICAL FAILURES

Like Lewis Carroll, another person—a politician—kept planning. The following list represents his career:

'31—failed in business
'32—defeated for legislature

'33—second failure in business
'36—nervous breakdown
'38—defeated for speaker
'40—defeated for elector
'43—defeated for Congress
'55—defeated for Senate
'56—defeated for vice president

In 1860 Lincoln was elected President of the United States.

It is important not only to keep planning, but to see the "failures" as stepping-stones. Getting unsuccessful plans out of the way leads to the formulation of successful ones. Do you have enough failed plans? When you do, you are close to an exciting success!

11

Metaphors for All Procedures

128. Radio Station WDEP

In the earlier listing of Reality Therapy, environment and procedures were taught as eight steps (N. Glasser, 1980). Alex Bassin, an instructor with the Institute for Reality Therapy, formulated a way to use and teach the first four steps: Involvement, Behavior, Evaluation, Planning. He suggested "IBEP" as a mnemonic useful in learning the delivery system for Reality Therapy. Now that the practice of Reality Therapy is seen in terms of procedures and environment, a different teaching analogy is necessary.

Both the procedures and environment are now seen as a "cycle of counseling" (Wubbolding, 1988) appropriately entered at any place. Thus, Glasser (1975) asks the "mental patient," "What's your plan?" before asking any other questions. Consequently, the procedures are not perceived or taught as steps to be followed in lock-step fashion. Therefore, Radio Station WDEP is a development of Bassin's ingenious idea, and is by far the most important of all metaphors. It is a way to both remember and implement Control Theory and Reality Therapy. As you read about WDEP, think of ways you can use it with others and ways to use it in your own life.

As a mnemonic or metaphor, WDEP is useful in understanding the most important procedures used in Reality Therapy. Each of the call letters refers to a cluster of strategies:

W = Wants: Help the person explore his/her wants, "the all we want world," "Picture Album," or the "Quality World." Related to this is the exploration of the "All we know world" or "the perceived world" and identifying the out of balance scales. Included as part of the "W" is sharing wants, i.e., telling the person what you want from them, such as to come to the appointment on time, give twenty-four hours' notice for cancellation, show up for work at 8:00 A.M., keep the curfew, study at 7:00 P.M., and other wants unique to each setting. Furthermore, the "W" implies getting a commitment and increasing it if possible (Wubbolding, 1988).

D = Direction and Doing: Discuss with the person where the Total Behavior is leading. Each element of Total Behavior can be discussed: acting, thinking, feeling, and physiology. Appropriate attention is given to each, but the emphasis is placed on the "doing" or "acting" aspect because the handle of the suitcase is attached to the "acting" part, i.e., we have more direct control over the "acting" than over the other elements of Total Behavior.

E = Evaluation: There are seven kinds of Evaluation

summarized in this single letter: 1) the effectiveness of the person's overall direction; 2) the effectiveness of specific "acting" behaviors; 3) the realistic possibility of attaining wants; 4) the helpfulness of specific perceptions; 5) the degree of expected success from the present level of client commitment; 6) the likelihood of the success of the plan: Is it a good plan? Does it fulfill the characteristics of a $\frac{SAMIC^3}{P}$ plan? 7) the self-evaluation of the helper—did the helper follow through, consult with another professional when necessary, and work within his/her limitations?

$P = Planning:$ This procedure is the most well-known and the goal of the counseling session. The plan should have characteristics as described in the metaphor $\frac{SAMIC^3}{P}$.

129. BEOWULF

The story of *Beowulf* illustrates how powerful the WDEP system can be. One Friday night, I visited a sister and her daughter, my niece who was a senior in high school. My niece and I took a long walk for about an hour. A very brief summary of the conversation is as follows (R = Bob, N = Niece):

R　How is school going?
N　It's going okay.
R　Have you thought about what you're going to do when you graduate?
N　Yes, I'd like to go into broadcasting.
R　That sounds great. What do you have to do to get there?
N　I'll need to do pretty well in school this year.
R　How do you think you'll do?

118

N   I'll need to get better grades.

R   How about this weekend? Do you have any homework?

N   (Disgusted) Yeah. I gotta read *Beowulf*.

R   Are you going to read it?

N   No, I don't feel like it.

R   If you don't read it what will happen to your grades?

N   They probably will go down.

R   If they go down, what effect will that have on getting into broadcasting?

N   It probably won't help.

The conversation was more lengthy, of course, but the above transcript contains the essence. On the next evening, my sister and niece came to my house. When my niece walked in the kitchen door, she blurted out the following statement:

"You'll be happy to know I read all my *Beowulf*."

The most notable element in this vignette is that at *no* time did I tell her what to do. Like most adolescents, she was aware of the adult's values and needed no lecture, sermon, or warning about the certain, irreparable, and catastrophic effects from failing to read *Beowulf*. I did not even push her to make a plan. The only procedures used were W-D-E. She made her own plan and read *Beowulf* immediately.

130. SWANS BY MATISSE

The theory and practice of Reality Therapy is deceptively simple. It is reminiscent of swans painted by Matisse. When he first painted swans, he painted photographic images of them. Every feather was exact. Only after painting swans for many years was he able to paint a magnificent swan with just a few strokes. Yet, in these few strokes, he captured the grace, elegance, and movement of the swan. So it is with Reality Therapy. Simplicity is not the same as easy.

131. STATIONARY HORSE ON THE MERRY-GO-ROUND

This metaphor is included to allow the reader to use your own ingenuity. There are many possible applications if the principles of behavior and perception as described in Control Theory are used. Some possible ideas that could be elaborated on are:

1. The horse seems to be moving and yet seems to be not moving. (Behavior)
2. The world around the horse appears to be moving. (Perception)
3. What kind of metaphorical plan could the horse make?

The reader is invited to describe other principles and to develop applications of the principles.

_____

_____

_____

_____

_____

_____

12

*Applying Metaphors
in Counseling*

This chapter is made up of two sections designed to apply metaphors to the counseling setting. Even though there is reference to "counselor" and "client," the ideas are equally applicable to family relations and to some work settings. Many readers at times serve as "counselors," "coaches," or "encouragers" to their children and employees. In the first section readers are asked to describe their own responses. The second section contains a transcript from a counseling session with a married couple. The skillful use of a primary and secondary metaphor serves as a backdrop to the use of the WDEP system.

I. PRACTICING METAPHORS
Below are listed several metaphors that hypothetical clients have used. In order to practice using meta-

phors and elaborating on their use in counseling, please note your response and incorporate the WDEP system and the use of the metaphor. The first example is already completed.

Cl. = Client. Cn. = Counselor.

1. Cl. "I feel like a floormat."
   Cn. "Would you like to get up from the floor?"
   Add your own responses. _____
   _____
   _____

2. Cl. "I'm down in the dumps today.
   Cn. _____
   _____
   _____

3. Cl. "I feel like a million bucks."
   Cn. _____
   _____
   _____

4. Cl. "I've been spinning my wheels."
   Cn. _____
   _____
   _____

5. Cl. "I'm on automatic pilot, but I don't know if I'm going up or down."
   Cn. _____
   _____
   _____

6. Cl. "My kid doesn't know up from down."
   Cn. _____
   _____
   _____

7. Cl. "My home is no picnic and my job is a pain, too. My kids are no bargain, either."

   Cn. _____

   _____

   _____

8. Cl. "I feel like I won the lottery."

   Cn. _____

   _____

   _____

9. Cl. "Changing my old habits is like climbing Mount Everest."

   Cn. _____

   _____

   _____

10. Cl. "My husband wants me to mother him."

   Cn. _____

   _____

   _____

11. Cl. "I don't want to burn my bridges."

   Cn. _____

   _____

   _____

12. Cl. "I'm between a rock and a hard place."

   Cn. _____

   _____

   _____

13. Cl. "My son acts like he's lost in space."

   Cn. _____

   _____

   _____

14. Cl. "He got caught with his pants down."

   Cn. _____

   _____

   _____

15. Cl. "My husband needs a vitamin for his attitude."

    Cn. _____
    _____
    _____

16. Cl. "Sometimes I think I'm right at the edge."

    Cn. _____
    _____
    _____

17. Cl. "She spends money like there's no tomorrow."

    Cn. _____
    _____
    _____

18. Cl. "Life seems stagnant to me."

    Cn. _____
    _____
    _____

19. Cl. "I was grounded."

    Cn. _____
    _____
    _____

20. Cl. "My blind date turned out to be a 'shipwreck.'"

    Cn. _____
    _____
    _____

Too often in counseling we are trained to paraphrase the words of the client. If a client says, "I feel like a floormat," the paraphraser says, "In other words, you feel people take advantage of you." This leap from the metaphorical, from the concrete to the abstract, is not necessary and often not helpful. The intent might be to show accurate empathy, but why is it necessary to change what the person says? Their words can be used as a lead-in for the effective use of Reality Therapy. Thus, a response could be any or all of the following:

1. How do people wipe their feet on you? Describe a situation that happened recently.
2. Does it help to be on the floor?
3. How would tonight be different for you if you were walking around instead of being on the floor?
4. How could you get up off the floor?
5. What will you do today to rise?
6. Do you want to change your "floormat" status?

The use of metaphors provides specific tools for counselors as well as ways to empathize or to see things from the perspective of the client and subsequently to help them search their behavioral suitcase for more effective actions.

II. *The Case of the Marriage Flu*
Below is part of a counseling session (third visit) containing an elaborated use of a metaphor. A couple with minor problems has sought help concerning their marriage.

W. = Wife H. = Husband Cn. = Counselor

Cn. We've talked several times now about how you argue and go your separate ways in your leisure time. I described your marriage as being a little sick. Have you thought any more about that?

W.	We did talk about it and were upset that you said that. But actually, you are right. It is sick.
H.	Do you think it is on the deathbed? We didn't think it was that bad when we started seeing you.
Cn.	What do you think now?
W.	I hope it's not that bad.
H.	Same here.
Cn.	I don't think it's dead or near death either. But it sounds like the analogy got you thinking.
H.	It sure did!
Cn.	(to wife) Do you agree?
W.	Absolutely!
Cn.	I'd say that the marriage has a case of the flu. It needs to be rehabilitated, but with care, it will probably recover.
H. and W.	"Flu" is a good way to describe it.
Cn.	How high is its temperature? 105 is too high, probably. 98.6 would mean that everything is fine.
H.	It's about 100 degrees.
W.	I'd go along with that.
Cn.	So you agree on a very important point, namely, the symptom. Are there any other symptoms that you can observe in this flu case?
H.	There is some tightness and congestion.
W.	I agree.

Cn. Do you understand why I am trying to get you to use an analogy, why I've encouraged you to think of your marriage as sick, as having the flu?

W. I'm not completely clear about it. But it's kind of fun to talk about it this way.

Cn. Sometimes using symbols helps to lessen the controversial part of the problem. In other words, you can be less emotionally upset about the problem and even talk about it in a playful way. After all, you've been tense about this and even had chills. This way of communicating can help you relax. Remember when we talked about lowering your perceptions? This is what you've been doing. Also, I want to ask you, has talking about the problem as you usually do helped to cure the flu?

W. No way! It made the situation worse.

H. I agree. It only makes the chills colder.

Cn. Then let's continue to think about the marriage in a different way and to talk about it metaphorically for a few minutes. When people have the flu, how do they treat it?

W. They call the doctor.

Cn. You've done that. Marriage flus are my specialty. What else do they do?

H. They take medicine.

W. They rest, too.

Cn. In other words, they begin to *do* things they were not doing, such as take medicine. And they *change* some things they were doing—from being active to taking it easy,

127

maybe even bed rest. Let's start with a discussion about changing some things—in other words, taking it easy.

W.   We've both been going at break-neck speed and now we need to rest.

Cn.   "Break-neck speed?" If that's the case, you're fortunate that your marriage only has the flu.

H.   Right, we could kill it if this kept up at this pace for a few more years.

Cn.   I agree. A case of the flu is a warning. It slows a person down, provides a reminder that we're not almighty, that we need to take care of ourselves and not be self-negligent. My mother used to tell me when I was in high school and I'd be going out in the winter, "Wear a hat." The flu is a reminder to wear a hat, to take care of yourself.

W.   (frowning) So the flu is a positive warning!

Cn.   I don't *like* the idea either. But the flu is better than pneumonia, cancer, or death.

W.   I see what you mean.

Cn.   You said you had chills also?

W. and H. (nodding in unison) Yes, definitely.

Cn.   So, in summary, we have here a mild case of the flu. There are three symptoms: 1) Fever of 100 degrees; 2)

	Congestion or tightness; 3) Chills. Is that accurate?
W. and H.	(nodding in unison) That's it.
Cn.	I like this description. And you both agree as to what the problem is. What do you think about this agreement?
H.	It's amazing that we agree.
W.	Yes. There's something happening here that I'm not clear on.
Cn.	Should I explain it?
H.	It might help.
Cn.	Using a figure of speech or metaphor to describe the marriage as having the flu has enabled you to change your perception of what the problem is. You see a problem that you can now work on. In the past, you thought that the other person ought to change. That resulted in blaming each other, finding fault, chilling the air, and congestion in the messages you gave each other. What effect did that kind of communication have on the relationship?
W.	It cooled off and we became angry at each other.
Cn.	Has your relationship changed even for a few minutes now as we sit here?
H.	I'd say I feel slightly better.
Cn.	I notice you smiled as you said that.
W.	I feel better but I wonder how long it will last.
Cn.	Let's not worry about how long it

will last. It's enough for now that you realize that life can be better. You now know what some good feelings are like.

W. You're right. It's a new experience for me.

Cn. Would you like to extend these few minutes of enjoyment to an hour, a day, or even longer?

H. Yes, for sure.

W. Yes, absolutely.

Cn. Okay. Let's go back to the symptoms. 1) 100-degree temperature or bad feelings toward each other; 2) congestion in your time spent together and even going at "break-neck speed" in opposite directions; and 3) chills in the communication. [*Note:* The counselor adds to the metaphor by attaching to each symbolic symptom a specific aspect of the marriage relationship which is out of balance. Clients rarely object to this subtle extension of the metaphor. In fact, having passed through the previous stage of using the metaphor exclusively, they now become ready to hear and deal with the three dysfunctioning aspects of the relationship. Also, as is quite typical, another metaphor (break-neck speed) is introduced. It serves no purpose to rigidly cling to only one metaphor. The use of many metaphors is quite helpful.]

W. How do we start? We've been *talking* about this. Let's *do* something.

H. Yes, let's take action.

Cn. You've been taking action—going in different directions. There's no need to rush into this.

H. But we can't keep talking and doing nothing.

Cn. I'm not sure you're ready for a lot of change.

W. If we don't get moving, this flu will get worse.

Cn. Before you jump into a flurry of activity, which, by the way, you've already tried, I'd like to ask you how hard you want to work at this rehabilitation from the flu.

H. I think we both want to work hard.

W. Of course.

Cn. Let's put it this way: Is this a commitment, a "maybe," "We'll try," "We might," or what?

H. You've asked us to read about the five levels of commitment (in the metaphor about trying to land an airplane). I want to do more than "try."

Cn. If the doctor said, "I'll try to call in a prescription to the druggist for your flu," what would you say?

W. I'd ask him about it. I'd want more than a weak effort. I'd want results.

Cn. In other words, your commitment is higher than merely trying.

H. Yes, we want to do whatever it takes.

Cn. (to wife) You're nodding. Is that your level of commitment, also?

W. Yes . . . whatever it takes.

Cn. We said your marriage has three symptoms of the flu. One of them is congestion and even "break-neck speed." What effect has this "break-neck speed" at which you're traveling had on the relationship?

W. It's torn us apart.

Cn. So maybe it won't be helpful to do more of the same.

W. What do you mean?

Cn. What about doing something different from what you've been doing?

H. We definitely need that. Maybe we need to slow down.

Cn. Exactly. If going 100 miles an hour in opposite directions has not helped bring you closer, how about slowing down? By the way, I have a hunch that you'll need to slow down, then stop, then change directions, and then you'll meet each other again.

W. How do we do that? It sounds overwhelming!

Cn. It's not as hard as it sounds. You said you were committed to working this out, didn't you?

H. Yes, we are.

Cn. Do you want to first slow down in order to get back together?

W. It would be a good idea.

Cn. Then I'd like to ask you about what you want from each other in the next week that would be a slow-down in your opposite directions? Who wants to go first? Keep in mind what you want from the other person is not a cure for the flu but only a small amount of medicine.

H. You go first.

W.   Okay. You know one thing that really gripes me is that when you come home from work, you always go to the mail first and look through it before you pay any attention to me.

H.   I like to get that out of the way. It seems so trivial.

Cn.   Is that what you do at work? Do you start with trivial tasks when you first arrive?

H.   No, I guess not. I've always told the people under me to do the important things first.

Cn.   Your wife has been getting a message here.

H.   I guess she's got the idea that I think she's less important than the mail.

W.   That's right.

Cn.   (to husband) What do you want from your wife that is on about the same level as what she said?

H.   Well, when we were first married, you used to volunteer to rub my back for two or three minutes when I'd come home. Now even when I ask, you don't seem to want to do it.

Cn.   You both have been going in opposite directions here. Or to put it another way, there is some congestion in the traffic. Has this resulted in some hard feelings?

W.   It makes the rest of the evening hard to bear.

H.   It's like we start off by being locked into the same coldness toward each other.

Cn.   So maybe if you can change some of the things you do, the bad feelings will be less. In other words, the fever will lessen. And the chills will disappear also.

W.   These symptoms are closely connected?

H.   I think I see something I did not see before.

Cn.   What is that?

H.   If we change one symptom, the others will change too.

Cn.   That's what happens in cases of the flu.

W.   Then, let's get moving.

Cn.   No need to go too fast. My concern is that if you go too fast, you'll go in different directions, and you are experts at that sort of thing.

H.   I see what you mean. But, can't we do something at least?

Cn.   If you insist. I want to be sure the congestion clears up and that you are going toward each other slowly so that you don't miss each other, or even crash into the other person.

H.   You love these analogies, don't you?

Cn.   Have they helped or hurt your marriage?

W.   Oh, they helped!

Cn.   I agree, now let's get back to what you want from each other early in the evening when you both arrive home from work. Once again, what impact does it have on the marriage flu symptoms when you go to the mail first and you refuse to give a back rub?

W. and H.	(in unison) The symptoms get worse.
Cn.	Higher fever and more chills?
W. and H.	(in unison) Yes.
Cn.	You're starting to agree to a lot of things. Maybe I was wrong about how fast we can proceed. Maybe you can make a lot of progress quickly.
W.	I think we both hope so.
Cn.	Since your behavior at home sometimes raises the fever and increases the chills, are you willing to change it immediately tonight?
H.	I'm willing to do it. It seems so easy—even trivial.
Cn.	It might be easy. (turning to wife) Would it be trivial to you?
W.	No, it would be a good start.
Cn.	You heard the saying, "Well begun is half done"?
H.	You have a million little sayings, don't you?
Cn.	Yogi Berra is my hero! But that quote is from another source, Plato, I believe.
W.	I guess it's my turn to commit. I'm willing to rub your back, even volunteer to do it.
Cn.	(to husband) What message did you hear in her tone of voice just now?
H.	That she's eager to do it, that she likes it.
Cn.	The thought just occurred to me that you both made the commitment to do

these plans without putting any contingency on them. You did not say that you would do it "on condition" that the other person does his or her plan.

H. What do you make of that?

Cn. I was going to ask you that question.

W. I think it means that we are truly committed to the marriage and to each other.

Cn. Exactly.

The above activity and the detailed example illustrate that metaphors can be brief or lengthy. Like any technique, they can be overused. If this occurs, the counselor will appear to be "playing mind games," and the result will be that efforts to help become neutralized. Metaphors are intended to facilitate counseling and communication. They are not ends in themselves.

Conclusion

This book contains metaphors useful in understanding the theory and practice of Reality Therapy. Some readers might say that many of the metaphors relate to life in general rather than to a particular counseling theory. This statement is totally true of several metaphors. It also could imply another fact: Reality Therapy concerns life. It is not a way of analyzing the past. Rather, it concerns the present, the here and now, and the controllable future. Paul Tillich, the German philosopher and theologian, defined reality as "that which we come up against—that which we adjust to, which does not adjust to us." And so Reality Therapy is based on the way healthy people cope with this "real world." This means we think about what we want and need and make attempts to get it. However, we don't deal directly with the world around us. We confront it through our senses, with our words, and by means of our thoughts . . . in other words, through metaphors.

APPENDIX

Reader Worksheet

The reader is invited to list two metaphors for each of the categories below and to describe why they were important and meaningful to you. This activity reinforces what you have learned about Control Theory and Reality Therapy.

A. *Metaphors for Needs*
   No. 1 _____   Why is it meaningful? _____
   No. 2 _____   Why is it meaningful? _____

B. *Metaphors for Wants*
   No. 1 _____   Why is it meaningful? _____
   No. 2 _____   Why is it meaningful? _____

C. *Metaphors for Behaviors*
   No. 1 _____ Why is it meaningful? _____
   No. 2 _____ Why is it meaningful? _____

D. *Metaphors for Perceived World and Perception*
   No. 1 _____ Why is it meaningful? _____
   No. 2 _____ Why is it meaningful? _____

E. *Environment*
   No. 1 _____ Why is it meaningful? _____
   No. 2 _____ Why is it meaningful? _____

F. *Metaphors for Direction and Doing*
   No. 1 _____ Why is it meaningful? _____
   No. 2 _____ Why is it meaningful? _____

G. *Metaphors for Evaluation*
   No. 1 _____ Why is it meaningful? _____
   No. 2 _____ Why is it meaningful? _____

H. *Metaphors for Planning*
   No. 1 _____ Why is it meaningful? _____
   No. 2 _____ Why is it meaningful? _____

AN INVITATION

The writing of this book is not yet completed, nor do I anticipate that I will ever stop collecting metaphors until I finally buy the farm, go to the happy hunting ground, pass on, get planted, kick the bucket, and meet my Maker.

Until then, I plan to continue to collect analogies, similes, figures of speech, vignettes, and anecdotes—all of which I have chosen to call metaphors. You are invited to send me any such metaphor which has been meaningful to you or which illustrates any aspect of human wisdom. If I use it you will be given credit for your contribution. Please send it, as well as any other inquiries, to:

Robert E. Wubbolding
Center for Reality Therapy
7777 Montgomery Road
Cincinnati, Ohio 45236
1-513-561-1911

BIBLIOGRAPHY

BARKER, P. *Using Metaphors in Psychotherapy.* New York: Brunner/Mazel, 1985.

BELKIN, G. *Contemporary Psychotherapies.* Chicago: Rand McNally, 1980.

BOORSTIN, D. *The Americans: The National Experience.* New York: Random House, 1965.

BOYD, T. *Skill Builder.* Charlotte, North Carolina: Ty Boyd Enterprises, 1990.

CLEMENS, S. *The Adventures of Tom Sawyer.* New York: Dodd, Mead, 1958.

COREY, G. *Issues and Ethics in the Helping Professions.* Pacific Grove, California: Brooks Cole, 1988.

COUSINS, N. *Anatomy of an Illness.* New York: Norton, 1979.

———. *The Healing Heart.* New York: Norton, 1983.

DESHAZER, S. "Brief Family Therapy: A Metaphorical Task." *Journal of Marital and Family Therapy,* Vol. 6, No. 4. In Selzer, L., *Paradoxical Strategies in Psychotherapy.* New York: John Wiley & Sons, 1986.

DREIKERS, R. *Maintaining Sanity in the Classroom.* New York: Harper & Row, 1971.

FAY, A. *Making Things Better by Making Them Worse.* New York: Hawthorn Books, 1978.

FLOYD, C. "Using the Car Analogy to Teach Control Theory to Gifted Elementary School Children." *Journal of Reality Therapy,* Vol. 7, No. 1, Fall 1987, 16–22.

FORD, E. *Permanent Love.* New York: Winston Press, 1979.

———. (1988). *Guarantee Love in Your Marriage* (videotape). Phoenix: Ford Pub.

———. Private Correspondence. 1988.

GLASSER, N. (ed.) *What Are You Doing?* New York: Harper & Row, 1980.

GLASSER, W. *Identity Society.* New York: Harper & Row, 1972.

———. *Glasser on Reality Therapy* (videotape set, series 3, tape 6). Los Angeles: Institute for Reality Therapy, 1975.

———. *Control Theory.* New York: Harper & Row, 1984.

———. *The Control Theory–Reality Therapy Workbook.* Los Angeles: Institute for Reality Therapy, 1986a.

———. *A Diagram of the Brain as a Control System.* Los Angeles: Institute for Reality Therapy, 1986b.

———. "Annual Address to the Institute for Reality Therapy," RT Convention, Kansas City, Missouri, 1989.

HILTON, C. *Be My Guest.* Englewood, New Jersey: Prentice-Hall, 1957.

LAKOFF, G. AND M. JOHNSON. *Metaphors We Live By.* Chicago: University of Chicago Press, 1980.

PASK, G. *The Cybernetics of Human Learning & Performance.* London: Hutchinson & Co., 1975.

PATTERSON, C. H. *Relationship Counseling.* New York: Harper & Row, 1974.

POWERS, W. *Behavior the Control of Perception.* New York: Aldine Publishing Co., 1983.

SELTZER, L. *Paradoxical Strategies in Psychotherapy.* New York: John Wiley & Sons, 1986.

STONE, I. *The Agony and the Ecstasy.* Garden City, New York: Doubleday, 1961.

———. *Passions of the Mind.* New York: Doubleday, 1971.

WEEKS, G. AND L. L'ABATE. *Paradoxical Psychotherapy: Theory and Practice with Individuals, Couples and Families.* New York: Brunner/Mazel, 1982.

WEINBERG, G. *Secrets of Consulting.* New York: Dorset House, 1985.

WEINER, N. *Cybernetics.* New York: John Wiley & Sons, 1961.

WOODY, R. *Fifty Ways to Avoid Malpractice.* Sarasota, Florida: Professional Resource Exchange, 1988.

WUBBOLDING, R. "Characteristics of the Inner Picture Album." *Journal of Reality Therapy,* Vol. 5, No. 1, Fall 1985, 28–30.

———. *Reality Therapy Training Manual.* Cincinnati: Center for Reality Therapy, 1986.

———. *Using Reality Therapy.* New York: Harper & Row, 1988.

———. *Evaluation.* Cincinnati: Real World Publications, 1990a.

———. *Reality Therapy and Family Counseling.* Cincinnati: Real World Publications, 1990b.

ZIGLAR, Z. *See You at the Top.* Los Angeles: Pelican Greiner, 1980.

———. *How to Stay Motivated* (audiotape series). Carrolton, Texas: Ziglar Corporation, 1989.

ABOUT THE AUTHOR

Robert E. Wubbolding is a professor of counseling at Xavier University in Cincinnati, Ohio. He is also director of the Center for Reality Therapy in Cincinnati and director of training at the Institute for Reality Therapy in Los Angeles. As a psychologist and licensed counselor he has taught Reality Therapy in North America, Europe, and Asia.

"He is one of my closest and most trusted associates. I couldn't recommend anyone more highly."

William Glasser, M.D.